"*Access and Release God's Peace* better time. Chaos and division are grappling for air space. Yet the Prince of Peace has already triumphed over every enemy we have. His peace dismantles the power and authority behind chaos. In doing so, it releases the Kingdom of God, enabling us to walk in the victory of Christ. This really is Paul Martini's life message. I highly recommend both the man and his message."

Bill Johnson, senior leader, Bethel Church, Redding, California; author, *The Way of Life* and *Raising Giant-Killers*

"*Access and Release God's Peace* by Paul Martini is a must read. God's Kingdom is commonly referred to as upside down. If that is true, then this peace that Jesus gives is a weapon of mass destruction against Satan and all his intentions. Paul perfectly communicates this and the power of ministering that peace of Christ and the impact it releases. It's an anointed book from an anointed man of God."

Robby Dawkins, film documentary subject, bestselling author and international conference speaker

"This book is a solid journey into brilliant facets of peace. It is carrying an impartation to experience the God of Peace, through courageous personal narrative, biblical truths and inspiring stories. I believe this book will be a catalyst for many people in pursuit of wholeness! I highly recommend it!"

Katie Luse, director, ConnectUp

"Paul has found unique grace keys to transforming futility and sorrow into peace and hope! It has been my delight to know him both as his pastor and as a receiver of the light he transmits. God's powerful peace is the antidote for offense, depression and despair. Read this book with expectation!"

Charles Stock, senior leader, Life Center
Ministries International

"Jesus tells us that if we truly love Him, then we'll obey Him. The Great Commission is not the Great Suggestion. It's my belief that without the peace of God, it's impossible to fulfill the Great Commission. Paul Martini is God's man to write this book. I'm excited for you to receive an impartation of peace as you read, and I know you will be strengthened to exercise that which crushes Satan under our feet. Paul will teach you not only how to possess peace, but how to weaponize peace and take back what the thief stole in the Garden."

Richie Seltzer, evangelist, Revivalist Culture

ACCESS AND RELEASE GOD'S PEACE

ACCESS AND RELEASE GOD'S PEACE

From Chaos and Confusion to Freedom and Power

PAUL MARTINI

Chosen

a division of Baker Publishing Group
Minneapolis, Minnesota

Published by Chosen Books
11400 Hampshire Avenue South
Bloomington, Minnesota 55438
www.chosenbooks.com

Chosen Books is a division of
Baker Publishing Group, Grand Rapids, Michigan

Printed in the United States of America

Library of Congress Cataloging-in-Publication Control Number: 2019017036

ISBN 978-0-8007-9942-7

Cover design by LOOK Design Studio

19 20 21 22 23 24 25   7 6 5 4 3 2 1

Contents

Foreword

In my years of ministry, from pastoring a small Baptist church to leading healing crusades all over the world, I have met countless pastors and leaders. Most leaders have a sense of calling and a desire to please God. Some of them have been through great hardship, some pastors walk in the miraculous, while others release great revelation from the Word of God. My friend Paul Martini is all these things and more. I have had the honor of watching him grow in life and ministry during his time with me at Global Awakening, where he now leads conferences around the globe. One of Paul's hallmark messages is the power of peace. And a powerful message it is. I have personally watched thousands touched by the revelation you will find in *Access and Release God's Peace: From Chaos and Confusion to Freedom and Power*.

For centuries, the Body of Christ has had a limited view of peace. Peace is more than the absence of conflict or a sweet, calm feeling on a stressful day. In the book of Romans, the apostle Paul defines the Kingdom of God as "righteousness, peace and joy in the Holy Spirit" (Romans

14:17), and our own Savior has chosen for Himself the title "Prince of Peace" (see Isaiah 9:6). Verses like these point toward a greater depth and mystery in the power of peace that our God offers to each one of us. In this book, Paul begins to unlock those hidden treasures that have been so long lost by the Church.

More than ever before, today's society is marked by constant distraction and frenetic busyness, even as reported cases of anxiety and other mental-health issues continue to rise. It seems few things are as revolutionary as a life lived in true peace. But Paul has done just that. He is a man who demonstrates the power of peace in both his ministry and his personal life. I have witnessed him in action on the mission field, from bringing emotional healing to hurting hearts to pulling people out of wheelchairs in South America. He also carries within him a deep peace that has endured some of the harshest trials a person can face.

Access and Release God's Peace explores many key aspects of God's peace, laying a solid foundation for how to walk in peace in your personal life and ministry. Paul's unique journey into peace gives him a one-of-a-kind perspective that he relates with engaging storytelling wrapped in powerful revelation. Paul explores how God's peace can be adapted to fit every situation in life, from the dramatic to the mundane. Peace can be found in the quiet confidence that puts a mother's heart at ease when she is tempted to fret over her backslidden son. Peace can comfort the father who is drowning in debt, unsure of how he can provide for his family. Peace can heal entrenched conflict between family members who have not spoken in decades.

But peace in every situation has one thing in common: Its true source and origin is in the person and work of Jesus Christ, who died on the cross to make our peace with God and rose from the dead so we would be empowered to walk in peace. Because of His work, we can live as justified peace ambassadors who know the Father and bring the Kingdom of peace to the earth. We are now commissioned as ministers of reconciliation with hearts aflame because of the Prince of Peace living within us and the Spirit of Peace working through us. It is with that goal in mind that I commend this book. All who read it will learn to walk in peace with the Prince of Peace.

Now is the time to take the step of faith and begin your journey toward peace. This decision can change your life, your family and your city, and it can bring you into a new dimension with God that you never thought possible. As you read, ask the Holy Spirit to lay a foundation of peace in your life. Then watch Him do just that. This book is a great crescendo to Paul's journey, and I look forward to seeing his continued fruitfulness in the years to come.

Paul's message in this book is a clarion call to the Body of Christ. The Father is beckoning His children to surrender their fears, cares, worries and fretting, and run to Him. In our surrender, we find true peace. There is no better time than now to begin your own peace revolution. Transform your life by encountering the all-powerful peace of your loving Father.

He is waiting for you.

You will not regret it.

Dr. Randy Clark, founder, Global Awakening

Introduction

If you asked me a few years ago what I envisioned my-self doing with my life, I certainly would not have said, "Preaching and teaching God's Word as I travel the world." My decision to leave a career in business management and pursue the life of a pastor was envisioned in the context of a local church setting.

Fast-forward a few years, and, armed with a B.A. in theology and two years of ministry school, I was offered a job as an associate pastor at a church in another state that I would often visit. It was a package deal that included a salary, a house and a car. *That's it.* I thought. *That's the Lord*—or so I thought. Shortly after this job offer, I received another offer from an internationally recognized healing ministry headed by Dr. Randy Clark.

Global Awakening invited me to come on staff and travel with Randy as his personal assistant. Initially, I turned the offer down because I thought working for a local church was the better way to go. Being a personal assistant to someone meant nothing more than carrying his or her bags and taking care of all the logistical details involved with life on the road. But God had other plans. In a dream, God spoke to me and made it clear that He wanted me to take the job with Global Awakening.

A Dream from God

In this dream, I was on the back of a motorcycle that Randy Clark was driving. We were speeding down a large highway at a hundred miles per hour—needless to say, I was holding on to Randy for dear life. Suddenly, in a split second, I was alone on an old Indian motorcycle, much like the kind found in World War II movies. The highway was gone, and I was driving on a dirt path that was becoming progressively narrower and more difficult to navigate. Eventually, I had to get off the bike and walk it through the woods.

As I walked through the woods, I came to a house. I entered the house through the garage and then went into the kitchen. I met a father figure there, a man I had known since the time I was sixteen years old. He had a big dog with him that proceeded to give me a big-dog welcome. As I petted and played with his dog, he said to me, "Paul, if you'll take this dog, I'll give him to you." Shocked and thankful, I agreed to take his dog.

Ditching my motorcycle, I continued my journey through the woods, but now, instead of riding the motorcycle, I was riding the dog. In the dream, I thought about how the journey was lonely but how I was thankful for the dog to get me where I needed to go.

The moment my eyes opened, I heard the Lord say, *Paul, that dream was from Me.* I immediately knew what the first part of that dream meant: I was to travel with Dr. Randy Clark. Even though I did not understand the entire dream at the time, I understood enough of it to know that God wanted me to take the job with Randy and Global Awakening. I immediately contacted them and said I would take the position if it was still available. I was thrilled, excited and scared all at the same time, because I knew God had something significant in store for me. He was mapping out a whole new trajectory for my life that would prove to be enormously formative, filled with rich mentoring and discipling by a humble man of God.

After traveling with Randy for two years, he invited me to speak at some of his conferences. It is an understatement to say that I was honored at the thought of sharing the platform with such gifted giants of the faith, spiritual heroes like Reinhard Bonnke, John Arnott, Heidi Baker, Cindy Jacobs, Bill Johnson, Randy Clark and many more. In fact, I was both honored and overwhelmed. *O God, help me*, I prayed. *What am I going to do? What am I going to teach after Randy has spoken? What am I going to say after Bill Johnson has shared the wisdom that You gave him? What do I have to offer that can even come close to what these amazing men and women of God walk in every day of their lives?*

In His grace, God clearly spoke to me: *Paul, I want you to share the message of your life.* In an instant, I knew exactly what He was talking about. The mess that God had brought me through—the difficulties I had endured—were now my testimony and the message God wanted me to share with those present. Up until that moment, I had always thought that the life lessons I had learned were just for me and my personal growth—something *I* was to carry, *my* journey with God. I never imagined that He would take my mess and turn it into a message for the benefit of others.

I want to encourage you that no matter what you are facing today, no matter what you are dealing with, God will take it and make it into a message that touches and changes lives—if you will let Him. Though it may not seem like it at the moment, God will get you through it, but He will do it not only for your own benefit but for the benefit of others. It will be a personal and powerful message that only you can give, because it is part of *your* journey with God, *your* story.

The message God has written on my heart and through my life is all about the power of His peace. Understanding the power of God's peace has changed my life on a personal level, and as I have traveled around the globe sharing this message with others, I have seen it change the lives of countless people who desperately needed to experience that peace. I am both humbled and grateful to share it with you in this book.

The Power of God's Peace

As I continually pressed into God to develop this message of peace, I quickly realized that God's concept of peace is far deeper and more multifaceted than I initially understood. As you read this book, I will seek to identify the lies and misconceptions we often entertain about the peace of God and define true peace that comes only from the Prince of Peace, Jesus Christ. Oftentimes, when we are stuck in a significant hardship or trial, it becomes so binding, painful and maybe even dark that we do not know how to break free. But God's peace is essential in overcoming our worst situations, and it brings us into a lifestyle of wholeness and victory. Once we are free from the constraints of chaos, we continue to move forward in bringing freedom to others. Peace does not mean we are passive; rather, peace is a weapon of advancement for the Kingdom of God that opens doors in the most difficult of areas. Peace is something that we can access so that we can give it away to others—it is not just for us. Just as God taught me lessons regarding peace so I could share those lessons with others, so God is inviting you to learn about Jesus as the Prince of Peace. As you find rest in Him, He will teach you how to bring peace to every situation you face, thus bringing God's Kingdom peace to those who are in need. Let me tell you one story before we get started.

I was in the middle of the airport not too long ago when I saw a woman struggling to carry her bags. She was using a cane and having great difficulty navigating through the airport with her luggage. While I watched her struggle, I felt God's compassion for her, so I went up to her and gently asked if she needed help. "Oh yes," she said, "but my gate is a good ten-minute walk from here." I had over an hour before my flight boarded, so off we went.

As we talked, I learned that Joy was on her way to see her children, whom she had not seen in quite a while. Needless to say, she was excited to see them. When we got to her gate, I told her I was a minister and offered to pray for her. "People sometimes get healed when I pray for them," I explained to her.

Born with a defect in her leg that prevented it from properly stretching out, she was forced to walk with a cane. She told me she did not know about God and did not have faith, so I began to explain to her that God's love for her surpasses any earthly love she might have known. This world is broken and not everything is God's will, I told her, including the issue with her leg. I explained to her about the peace of God that He wants to bring into this broken world through Jesus Christ. I then asked if I could pray for God to bring peace to her body.

With her permission, I laid my hand on her shoulder and prayed a quick prayer. I asked for her body to come into order with the peace of God and that everything Jesus paid for on the cross would manifest in that moment. As I prayed, I could feel the power of God flow through my hands, bringing peace into her body and into the atmosphere that surrounded us. I asked her to check out her leg to see if she could do anything with it that she could not do before. When she did, she found she was able to straighten it out for the first time in her life.

In disbelief, she started walking and then jumping up and down, right there in the airport. It was easy to lead her to the Lord. In the middle of the airport, she received Christ as her Savior. The Prince of Peace brought Joy into real peace that day. She only had one complaint, though: She wanted to know why I made her walk to her gate with her bad leg before I prayed with her.

Joy went on her way, eager to get home and show her healed leg and her new life to her children. God is so good.

The peace that God brings is a supernatural confirmation of the presence of God that is bringing power and wholeness to the believer in every section of his or her life.

The Invitation

I invite you to journey with me now on the path to God's peace as we know it in the person of Jesus Christ. No matter what your circumstances are today, Christ in you, who is the hope of glory, will empower you to walk through this life with His peace that passes all understanding. We can truly embody the words of the apostle Paul when he writes, "Do not be anxious about anything, but in every situation, by prayer and petition, with thanksgiving, present your requests to God. And the peace of God, which transcends all understanding, will guard your hearts and your minds in Christ Jesus" (Philippians 4:6–7). As the people of God, we have been extended a tremendous invitation to partner with God in His peace, allowing us to access it and then give it away to others.

■ 1 ■

Getting Personal

You hem me in behind and before, and you lay your
hand upon me. Such knowledge is too wonderful for
me, too lofty for me to attain.

Psalm 139:5–6

I know what it is like to live without God's peace and
to experience pain in this life. Just because I experience
God's peace now in a greater measure does not mean it
has always been that way. When I was just nineteen years
old, I married my high-school sweetheart. Early in our
marriage, our beautiful and amazing twins were born.
Both my wife and I grew up in Christian homes, but our
faith was nominal Christianity at best.

Throughout our marriage, we attended church as a family, but it became more of a routine than a way of life for
us. I worked full-time while she mainly stayed at home and
took care of the kids. By any means, I was not a perfect

21

husband. In fact, looking back on my life from where I now stand, I was a really broken person. I am pretty sure I was tough to live with, stubborn and totally lost, so I can see why my wife was not happy with our relationship. But I was faithful, and I was never physically or verbally abusive to her or the kids.

As my wife began walking through some difficult circumstances in her own life, we became vulnerable and our relationship became quite strained. The enemy saw the opening and went for it. He took every weakness and small crack in our foundation and turned them into the biggest chasm he possibly could. Things began to come apart, and before long the unthinkable happened. I came home one day and learned that my wife no longer loved me and did not want to be with me. My life and the lives of our two young children would never be the same again.

I was absolutely and totally crushed. In one moment, my life was turned upside down. I went from seeing my children every day to hardly seeing them at all. My days were consumed with fighting for my family and my children. But I lost. With the way the laws were, especially in the state where I lived, it was a long time before I was able to see my children in any kind of consistent way. I know why God hates divorce (see Malachi 2:16): It is because nobody wins—not the father or the mother, and especially not the children.

Hurting and broken, I ran as far as I could into the world. I worked a nine-to-five white-collar job and made friends with the world. I began drinking to numb the pain and the heartache I felt. I would not say I became an alcoholic, but I definitely drank like one. One night, when nobody was around, I remember sitting in the basement of my rental home drinking wine out of the bottle. You know you are pretty low when you are drinking wine out of a bottle instead of a nice wine glass. It was a desperate, rock-bottom moment that brought me to my knees.

"Help me, God," I cried out. As my words faded, His presence filled the room. Suddenly, I did not want to run any longer. It was time to stop and take a hard look at the way I was living my life.

God and I talked that night. In my ignorance of who He was, I recall telling Him that although He would never use me because I was such a failure, at least I could aim to be a good person. From that day on, I began cleaning up my act. I moved back in with my parents, which, as an adult man, is not the greatest experience in the world. Reliving your teenage years with an Italian mom can be brutal at times, but it was good to be home. My parents loved me and supported me. I went back to church, which also helped. Then came my favorite holiday.

'Cause of Jesus

Thanksgiving is my favorite holiday because no one expects anything from you, especially if you are a man in my family. Everyone in the family gets together, you eat as much food as you can, you hang out, you watch football, you fall asleep in front of the TV and then wake up and eat dessert. If you are a guy, holidays cannot get much better than that.

Most places are closed on Thanksgiving evening, except for the bars, which always seem to be open. After my post-Thanksgiving nap, the ache in my heart for my children hit me hard, so I slipped away and headed for a nearby bar. Like most bars, it was dark inside. On this particular Thanksgiving evening, there were only two other guys in there, sitting at the end of the bar, sipping red wine as they talked. Ignoring them, I sat at the other end of the bar and ordered a shot and a pint of beer.

When the bartender put them down in front of me, I immediately drank them both. Then I ordered another and immediately drank those too. Figuring that was enough alcohol for the moment, I grabbed a pack of cigarettes from the vending machine and went outside for a smoke. It is pretty depressing to be on the sidewalk, leaning on the window of a bar on Thanksgiving Day, while smoking a cigarette. But there I was, wallowing in my sorrows, smoking a cigarette and believing the lie that nothing in my life would ever change, that I would never find true peace.

One of the guys from the bar came outside, pacing back and forth while talking on his cell phone. When he finished his conversation, he was about to walk back inside, but something stopped him. Where I am from, you do not pay attention to people you do not know, so I pretended to ignore him. As he went through the door, he stopped, looked at me and said, "Are you going to make it?"

"What?" I asked him, trying to ignore his words.

"You heard me," he said. "Are you going to make it?"

"Yeah," I replied, totally caught off guard.

"How do you know?" he asked me.

"'Cause of Jesus," I blurted out, instantly embarrassed because it felt like the kind of default answer kids give when they are in Sunday school and do not know the correct answer to the teacher's question.

"Jesus?" he replied. "Why did you say *Jesus?*"

Still stumbling around in a verbally challenged moment, I tried another way to say it: "'Cause I'm a Christian," I said.

"What's your name?" he asked me.

"My name is Paul."

"Wow, you know, Paul in the Bible did amazing things for God," he told me. "One day, Paul, you're gonna do amazing things for God too." After he said that, he walked back into the bar. The conversation was over.

I threw my cigarette down, ran to my car and sat there bawling. God was speaking to me. He was with me. In fact, God was chasing after me. He wanted me to experience His redemption. He wanted me to experience true peace that comes only from Him. No matter how dark or desperate your situation is today, God can and will find you. And when He does find you, He will release His peace to you—if you will receive it.

Discovering God's Peace

The psalmist tells us that God is present in all of our circumstances, during our best days and during our worst ones. In fact, there is no place we can go where He cannot find us and where He will not pursue us. He is intimately acquainted with all of our ways, knowing even our deepest thoughts. He is the One who formed us in our mother's womb, so He knows us inside and out. David writes, "You have searched me, LORD, and you know me. You know when I sit and when I rise; you perceive my thoughts from afar. You discern my going out and my lying down; you are familiar with all my ways" (Psalm 139:1–3). He then continued:

> Where can I go from your Spirit? Where can I flee from your presence? If I go up to the heavens, you are there; if I make my bed in the depths, you are there. If I rise on the wings of the dawn, if I settle on the far side of the sea, even there your hand will guide me, your right hand will hold me fast.
>
> Psalm 139:7–10

It is important to remember that all of us experience storms in this life. There is not one person born on this planet who is exempt from them. But it is how we respond to those storms that determines the outcome of our lives. We can try to navigate life's choppy waters on our own, or we can navigate them in the power of God's peace. On our own, we are vulnerable to the wind and the waves, but with the empowering peace of God in us, we will get to the other side despite the storms we face. We can either be an overcomer or we can be overcome by what life brings to us. The choice is ours.

From the moment I had the conversation with the man outside the bar on Thanksgiving, I started the journey of discovering God's peace and found it more than sufficient to sustain me through any storm that comes to challenge the destiny over my life. God wants you to experience His peace too. It is available to everyone who believes on the name of Jesus, not only for a select few or those who are super spiritual. God's peace is available for every single person who trusts in Christ as his or her Savior and Lord.

A Life of Supernatural Peace

In the Scriptures, we find Jesus teaching what it looks like to live in the power and victory of God's peace. Jesus gave His disciples peace that overcomes the world, saying, "I have told you these things, so that in me you may have peace. In this world you will have trouble. But take heart! I have overcome the world" (John 16:33), and again, "Peace I leave with you; my peace I give you. I do not give to you as the world gives. Do not let your hearts be troubled and do not be afraid" (John 14:27). But Jesus also lived a life of supernatural peace, demonstrating that we can both access and release His powerful peace.

While Jesus and His disciples were crossing a lake one day, a great storm arose and the disciples were afraid that they were going to drown. If we are honest with ourselves, many times we feel much the same way in our circumstances: "Jesus, don't you care if we drown?" (see Mark 4:38). Does He even care what we are going through? Does He see our lives and how hard they are? But where was Jesus in the midst of the storm? He was sleeping, because He lived a life of abundant peace that was not swayed by the circumstances in this world. He lived a life of perfect trust in His Father, letting the Father's peace pervade His soul in the midst of the chaos that surrounded Him. And when He woke up, He spoke peace over the wind and the waves, and they immediately calmed (see Mark 4:35–41).

Just like the disciples, you, too, can learn from Jesus what it means to live in the supernatural peace that only He offers. Jesus sees you, He knows you and He understands and sympathizes with what you are going through. He is the One who is with you in the midst of the storm, speaking peace to all of your chaotic circumstances: "Quiet! Be still!" (Mark 4:39). We have access to God's supernatural and powerful peace through the Prince of Peace, Jesus Christ.

▪ PRAYER FOR PEACE ▪

Father, help me to see what it would look like to live a life of peace. Help me to see that Your peace is so much more powerful and effective than the so-called peace this world offers to me. Jesus, You said, "I have told you these things, so that in me you may have peace" (John 16:33). Even though I am not immune to the storms of life, I can live knowing that You give me peace in the midst of chaos, and that I can speak to the storms of my life and calm will reign in the midst of turmoil. I command all of my circumstances to be submitted to the rule of Your peace today. Help me to see that You are passionately pursuing me with Your peace. I surrender to Your pursuit today. In the name of Jesus, I pray. Amen.

■ 2 ■

Peace Is Powerful

The God of peace will soon crush Satan under your feet.

Romans 16:20

When it comes to the topic of peace, most believers walk around with a little bit of head knowledge and even less heart knowledge. We sing songs about peace, hear sermons on peace and say to each other, "Peace to you," but do we really know what peace means or what to do with it? A lot of our struggle has to do with a misunderstanding of the word *peace* in the context of Jesus' life and teachings.

If we have no faith in the power of peace, then that power cannot change us or impact our lives in any way. When we live convinced that peace is powerful, however, that conviction will open the door to empowered Christian living. The apostle Paul understood this concept well. In Romans 16:20, he writes, "The God of peace will soon crush Satan under your feet." Paul understood the place peace has in living the empowered Christian life in a fallen world. Let us unpack a couple of nuggets of wisdom from this verse so we can learn how powerful peace truly is.

The God of Peace

Throughout the Bible, the names of God are used to reveal the nature of His being. God also uses different words and terms to describe Himself throughout Scripture. In this verse, Paul calls God the "God of peace." This is an amazing title that reveals to us the importance and power of God's peace in our lives. He does not call Him the God of power, although He is all-powerful; he does not call Him the God of love, although God is love and embodies love; rather, Paul refers to God as the God of peace. He understands the connection between God's peace and His power: "The God of peace will soon crush Satan under your feet" (Romans 16:20).

There is something else Paul communicates here, and that is the positional aspect of God's peace. When Jesus defeated His enemies through His death on the cross and His subsequent resurrection, God put them as a footstool under His feet, symbolizing total victory and authority over all existence. Paul reminds us of this when he writes, "And having disarmed the powers and authorities, [Jesus] made a public spectacle of them, triumphing over them by the cross" (Colossians 2:15). The power of God's peace at work in your life will bring your enemies into total submission, enabling you to walk in victory in the most difficult of circumstances. In fact, the power of this peace will actually bring order where the enemy has created chaos.

If all this sounds too good to be true, it is because there is a difference between God's peace and the peace the world offers to us, as most people understand it. Worldly thinking tends to see peace as the absence of conflict and as something that is weak and easily broken. For example, if two countries sign a peace treaty, one bullet fired from a gun can quickly break that agreement. That is why, when it comes to maintaining peace in this world, many walk on eggshells with an underlying anxiety just to maintain a semblance of peace.

As a child, I constantly heard my parents say, "Don't rock the boat." That was their way of telling my siblings and me to do whatever was needed to keep things from getting out of control in our behavior toward each other. It is a bit like saying, "Take the brunt of the problem so the other person does not have to." That is worldly peace, which really is not peace at all. God's peace looks quite different from this type of peace.

God's peace is not the absence of conflict. Instead, God's peace overcomes and transcends all conflict. His peace creates order out of chaos and brings us and our situations into full redemption. God's peace is not about us emptying ourselves so we experience a mindless tranquility; it is about filling all of us with all of Him. To the world, peace is only a concept. But for believers, peace is a tangible anointing that comes from the Holy Spirit. This is why Paul reminds us to "let the peace of Christ rule in [our] hearts" (Colossians 3:15), and Peter tells us to "cast all [our] anxiety on him because he cares for

[us]" (1 Peter 5:7). Peace is powerful and alters the way we live our lives.

Righting All Wrongs

Because peace fundamentally has power within it, when we pray for peace over a person, we are not asking God to make him or her quiet down and be still and accept difficult circumstances with tranquility. We are actually asking the Holy Spirit to come and make right all that is wrong in that person's life—to bring healing to that person's situation, to bring restoration to his or her body and to bring order to that chaos.

I was in Canada speaking at a small revival meeting a few years ago. While making my way to the front of the sanctuary, I walked past a woman in the back of the room who was lost in worship, her hands raised to heaven. As I passed by her, I felt God's compassion for her, but I quickly went to my seat in the front where the speakers sit so I could start worshiping too. As I started to sing and pray and prepare for the service, however, the Lord nudged me to go back to the woman and pray for her. Out of obedience, I stopped worshiping and went back to find her, not knowing if she even needed prayer. I did not really know what to say, so I simply asked her if she would like prayer.

When God leads us to pray for a person, we do not need to be extra spiritual or try to guess what that person needs. If God leads us to pray for someone but does not tell us what to specifically pray for, then we only need to ask the person what he or she needs prayer for. This woman had serious health issues. She had constant migraines and ringing in her ears, causing her to often feel dizzy. All of these issues were seriously impacting her day-to-day life. With her permission, I laid my hands on her head and ears, and I prayed for God's healing to take place in her body. But more importantly, I asked God to bring His peace into her life.

At first, nothing seemed to happen, so I continued to pray. Then, with my hands touching her head softly, I began to feel a calm, confident and strong surge of God's presence flow through my hands and into her head. It was peaceful but powerful. She started to weep and then fell to her knees. I gently kept my hands on her head as the power of God continued to flow into her body. She began to sweat profusely from the anointing of God's presence.

"How are you feeling?" I asked her. "What's happening?"

"They're gone," she said. "The headaches are gone, and the dizziness has ceased."

God healed her. This dear woman experienced the powerful peace of God crushing sickness under His feet. His peace was tangible. It was felt. I felt it, and she experienced it as physical heat and healing in her body. God's peace came on the scene and sickness had to submit, just as the wind and the waves submitted at the command of Christ (see Mark 4:35–41). There is power contained in God's peace: "The God of peace will soon crush Satan under your feet" (Romans 16:20).

Pursuing God's Peace

As we journey together into a greater understanding of the peace of God that passes all understanding, know that this kind of peace in your daily life is an accessible, tangible and powerful anointing that is available to all believers. When you live convinced of this truth—of the power of God's supernatural peace—then you will pursue it much more eagerly, realizing how important it is to the Christian life. In fact, accessing and releasing the peace of God is foundational for Christian living. We cannot truly live out all God has destined for us if we do not know how to access God's supernatural peace. It is essential to discipleship.

Paul closed his letter to the Philippians by making this connection between the power of God's peace and faithfully living the Christian life:

> Rejoice in the Lord always. I will say it again: Rejoice! Let your gentleness be evident to all. The Lord is near. Do not be anxious about anything, but in every situation, by prayer and petition, with thanksgiving, present your requests to God. And the peace of God, which transcends all understanding, will guard your hearts and your minds in Christ Jesus.
>
> Finally, brothers and sisters, whatever is true, whatever is noble, whatever is right, whatever is pure, whatever is lovely, whatever is admirable—if anything is excellent or praiseworthy—think about such things. Whatever you have learned or received or heard from me, or seen in me—put it into practice. And the God of peace will be with you.
>
> Philippians 4:4–9

Faithfully giving witness to the God of peace means that when we experience anxiety and trouble in this world, we turn to God in prayer. And as we commune with God in our daily lives, then the "peace of God, which transcends all understanding, will guard [our] hearts and [our] minds in Christ Jesus." What a wonderful promise of the power of God's peace to change our lives and influence the way we live out the Gospel. As we put what we learn into practice, "The God of peace will be with [us]." He is with us, transforming our Christian experience by the power of His peace.

Identify those places in your life where you have allowed chaos to rule, and then ask yourself if you believe God's peace has the power to change your situation. God's peace is supernatural, and it is powerful. Remember, the "God of peace will soon crush Satan under your feet" (Romans 16:20). Here is a prayer for you to have an increase of faith for God's peace to be activated in your life.

▪ PRAYER FOR PEACE ▪

Father, I ask that You bring Your powerful peace into my life. I want to feel Your tangible, peaceful presence flow over me like a river. Come, Holy Spirit, and anoint me with the peace of heaven, and break the strongholds of anxiety, stress and torment. Flood my soul until it overflows like a river gushing out of my belly with the peace of heaven. May Your powerful peace overcome and transcend any physical, emotional or spiritual chaos in my life. I command all distractions from the realities of God to go, in Jesus' name. I command my mind, body and spirit to break free from the spirit of trauma and move into full restoration. I thank You that You are the God of peace. Help me to access and live in the abundance of Your peace today. Thank You, Jesus. Amen.

◾ 3 ◾

Peace Is Central
to the Gospel

"I will make a covenant of peace with them and rid
the land of savage beasts so that they may live in the
wilderness and sleep in the forests in safety."

Ezekiel 34:25

A careful reading of the Scriptures reveals that the message
and major theme for humanity contained in the Bible is
that God is restoring peace regarding the covenant between Him and His people. When God sought to renew
His covenant with Israel after they had been carried away
to Babylonian captivity, for example, He said, "I will make
a covenant of peace with them; it will be an everlasting
covenant. I will establish them and increase their numbers, and I will put my sanctuary among them forever"
(Ezekiel 37:26). And God promises us in Isaiah, "Though

the mountains be shaken and the hills be removed, yet my unfailing love for you will not be shaken nor my covenant of peace be removed" (Isaiah 54:10).

The covenant of peace is a promise that is threaded throughout all of Scripture, from the Old Testament to the New Testament. In fact, I would even say that the covenant of peace is central to the Gospel, because, through His death and resurrection, Jesus reconciled humanity to the Father, thus restoring peace in our relationship with God and with one another. "God was pleased," wrote Paul, "to reconcile to himself all things . . . by making peace through his blood, shed on the cross" (Colossians 1:19–20).

The Gospel is not just that our sins are forgiven and we are assured of heaven when we die—though Jesus provided for these realities. The Gospel is also about those realities giving us real-world peace: peace in our relationship with God and in our relationships with each other, peace in our bodies and in our souls, peace in the chaotic situations that are contrary to God's will. This experience of real-world peace is one of the reasons Paul could write with confidence:

> Therefore, since we have been justified through faith, we have peace with God through our Lord Jesus Christ, through whom we have gained access by faith into this grace in which we now stand. And we boast in the hope of the glory of God. Not only so, but we also glory in our sufferings, because we know that suffering produces perseverance; perseverance, character; and character, hope. And hope does not put us to shame, because God's love

has been poured out into our hearts through the Holy Spirit, who has been given to us.

Romans 5:1–5

We can "boast in the hope of the glory of God" in our present circumstances, no matter what situations we face today, because we have "peace with God through our Lord Jesus Christ." Through the Gospel, Jesus provided peace with the Father, which affects how we live our present life, granting us to "access by faith into this grace in which we now stand."

In *Peace in Paul and Luke*, New Testament scholar Michael J. Gorman confirms the connection of peace being central to the Gospel. He suggests that the goal of God found throughout Scripture is to restore His peace to humanity. What we forfeited in the Garden of Eden through the first sin, God has graciously restored in and through Christ. The restoration of His peace comes to us as a covenant that He keeps with us through Jesus Christ. Scripture quickly makes it obvious that peace is of great importance to God because He mentions it so often, particularly in the New Testament. Its significance is not only determined by the number of times peace is mentioned in the Bible, but also by its location and connection to other words and themes.[1]

For this reason, it is important that we look at the overarching picture of peace as it is communicated in Scripture. At its core, the Gospel is a message of peace, presenting Jesus as the promised Messiah who would reconcile God and humanity and bring ultimate peace to our lives. And then we access that covenant of peace through continual communion with and immersion in Him.

Salvation and Peace

We are not born into peace; rather, we are each born into sin and chaos with lives that are marred by strife, confusion and grief. We are fractured, we are broken, we are shattered and we remain so without Christ. Our emotions, our minds and our spirits have been depraved since the Fall of Adam and Eve in the Garden of Eden. Lacking freedom, we live a sinful life that is blinded by the world, not knowing true salvation or lasting peace. Essentially, we are lost without even knowing we are lost. The salvation offered to us by Christ, however, through His death and resurrection, is so much more than only receiving a confidence that we are going to heaven when we die. Salvation in Christ restores God's covenant of peace that brings freedom from bondage and healing to our souls, empowering us to live a victorious life.

In the Hebrew Scriptures, the simple yet powerful meaning of *shalom* is completeness or wholeness that is paid for, or that is paid for in advance.[2] Likewise, the word *salvation* in the New Testament is the Greek word *sozo*, which means healed, saved, delivered and ultimately restored. *Sozo* suggests that salvation is all-encompassing, touching every area of body, soul and spirit.[3] Not only that, but salvation is also spoken of as being a past reality, a present experience and a future hope.

Paul writes that salvation has already taken place and is currently taking place, and he also sees it as taking place in the future. For example, in Ephesians 2:8–9, Paul writes, "For it is by grace *you have been saved*, through faith— and this is not from yourselves, it is the gift of God—not by works, so that no one can boast" (emphasis added). Salvation is a past event for those who have received Christ as their Savior. But in 1 Corinthians 1:18, Paul writes of salvation as a present reality: "For the message of the cross is foolishness to those who are perishing, but to us *who are being saved* it is the power of God" (emphasis added). That is to say, we are presently in the process of being saved. And finally, for Paul, our final salvation is rooted in a future hope: "Since we have now been justified by his blood, how much more *shall we be saved* from God's wrath through him" (Romans 5:9, emphasis added).

When taken together, these two words—*shalom* and *sozo*—reveal a wonderful aspect and a more complete picture of our salvation in Christ: He becomes our peace, bringing health, salvation and wholeness to every area of our lives, in the past, now in this present life and in the future that is to come. The salvation (*sozo*) that is available in and through Jesus gives us real and lasting peace (*shalom*), causing us to become whole and restored.

We are now at peace with God because Jesus became our atoning sacrifice, giving us access to the Father, as originally intended when God created humanity in the Garden of Eden. Like Adam and Eve before the Fall, we, too, can experience unhindered intimacy with God through the peace that Jesus provided for us through His death and resurrection. Coming into the fullness of our salvation is a continuing process that unveils this access, granting us entrance to our birthright to walk in the peace of God. Not only do we have total peace in Christ, but Jesus has become our peace, reconciling us to the Father and to one another.

41

He Is Our Peace

Paul wrote about this wonderful peace we have in Jesus that comes through His death and resurrection—through the good news of the Gospel. When Jesus arose from the grave, He became our peace, conquering the chaos of sin that used to rule us. Paul wrote that the Father "has rescued us from the dominion of darkness and brought us into the kingdom of the Son he loves, in whom we have redemption, the forgiveness of sins" (Colossians 1:13–14). Just a few sentences later, Paul writes, "For God was pleased to have all his fullness dwell in him, and through him to reconcile to himself all things, whether things on earth or things in heaven, by making peace through his blood, shed on the cross" (Colossians 1:19–20). It was Jesus' shed blood on the cross that reconciled us to the Father, thus giving us true and lasting peace.

So, it is only through the Gospel—the restoration of God's covenant of peace—that we obtain real peace. Through the cross, this peace is established between us and God, but it is also worked out in our relationships with others. In fact, the racial enmity that Jews and Gentiles experienced toward each other was overcome through the cross, with both of them becoming one new person in Christ. Paul reminded us of this fact when he wrote:

> For He Himself is our peace, who has made both one, and has broken down the middle wall of separation, having abolished in His flesh the enmity, that is, the law of commandments contained in ordinances, so as to create in Himself one new man from the two, thus making peace, and that He might reconcile them both to God in

one body through the cross, thereby putting to death the enmity.

Ephesians 2:14–16 NKJV

Jesus' supernatural peace was released through His sacrifice, breaking down the barriers that divided different classes of people. Paul writes again:

So in Christ Jesus you are all children of God through faith, for all of you who were baptized into Christ have clothed yourselves with Christ. There is neither Jew nor Gentile, neither slave nor free, nor is there male and female, for you are all one in Christ Jesus. If you belong to Christ, then you are Abraham's seed, and heirs according to the promise.

Galatians 3:26–29

Through the cross, Jesus provided for the reconciliation of all of humanity to the Father, thus establishing the possibility of peace with God and peace with one another. Without reconciliation with the Father through the blood of Jesus, we would have no peace at all. True and lasting peace, with God and with others, only comes through the good news of the Gospel. It cannot come in any other way. If peace is so essential to the Kingdom of heaven and that important to God, then it needs to be that important to us. But how do we continually access this peace on a practical level?

A Healthy Spiritual Diet

There is a verse in Romans that suggests that the Kingdom of heaven is, at least partially, made up of peace. Paul

43

writes, "For the kingdom of God is not a matter of eating and drinking, but of righteousness, peace and joy in the Holy Spirit" (Romans 14:17). In this one sentence, Paul gives us insight into what makes up a healthy spiritual diet. This world is not merely comprised of physical objects that we can taste and touch and smell. It is not enough to only eat and drink to nourish the physical body; we need to recognize the spiritual component of our lives and nourish that as well. When it comes to the Kingdom, spiritual nourishment is righteousness, peace and joy in the Holy Spirit. Through the Holy Spirit, we have the sufficient nutrients available to feed our spirits. If we do not have peace and we do not experience that peace, then we are lacking a major spiritual macronutrient.

Have you ever gone on a diet, maybe an extreme one? Many times, when we go on extreme diets, we end up cutting out essential nutrients, which limits our performance. Often, we become physically fatigued and our brain is foggy for much of the day. Our body cannot properly perform because we limited a major nutrient that it relies on to function. Sometimes, people cut out so much meat from their diet and do not supplement it with natural greens that they lack iron, which is a major nutrient. As such, their bodies greatly suffer because they are deficient in iron.

Similarly, when we live our spiritual lives and do not have peace residing within us, it is like cutting out a major nutrient that our spiritual bodies crave. In order to eat and retain what feeds our spirit, we need to be in communion with the Lord and fellowship with the Holy Spirit. It is not enough to pray that we receive peace as if we are ordering food from a fast-food restaurant, which is the experience many believers have when they need peace. We often ask God for peace but are not willing to stay in communion with Him long enough to fully experience it.

We need to take up residence and spend time with the giver of peace so that when we go into the world, we smell like the atmosphere of the One we reside in. It may sound simple, but embracing and digesting God's peace can be a huge challenge in the midst of our busy lives. And yet we are called to let the peace of Christ rule in us (see Colossians 3:15). But how do we do that?

Immersion in Christ

If we are to be immersed in Christ, and thus let His peace rule in our hearts, it is not enough to do quick visits with God when we are in need of some immediate peace. It takes full immersion into His manifest presence if we are to live lives that are characterized by peace. This means that we allow God to take up residence in our hearts so that we are talking and listening to Him at all times and in everything that we do. It is no coincidence that Paul talks about the peace of Christ ruling in our hearts in the context of our daily living and worship:

> Let the peace of Christ rule in your hearts, since as members of one body you were called to peace. And be thankful. Let the message of Christ dwell among you richly as you teach and admonish one another with all wisdom through psalms, hymns, and songs from the Spirit, singing to God with gratitude in your hearts. And whatever you

do, whether in word or deed, do it all in the name of the Lord Jesus, giving thanks to God the Father through him.

Colossians 3:15–17

I grew up in an Italian family in the Philadelphia area. My Italian parents loved to cook, which meant that our mealtimes were always full of family and friends. We ate all the time and constantly fellowshiped with the community around us. My parents were locally known for making amazing meatballs that were in constant demand.

I still remember the day my friends in middle school asked me if my family owned a meatball sandwich shop. When I told them we did not and asked them why they had asked, I was shocked to learn that sometimes my clothes and hair—my whole body!—smelled like a meatball sub. I was so immersed in my family culture that I had no awareness that I carried a particular scent. I wear a lot of cologne to this day because of my fear of smelling like meatballs. But the point is that we will exude the atmosphere we are around the most.

Immersion in Christ—constantly living connected to Him and in fellowship with Him—means that we live in and are a part of a place and culture so much like Jesus that we become a fragrant aroma of heaven. We smell like the atmosphere we came from. Instead of ordering peace from God like fast food, allow the One who is the source of peace to take up residence within you. Become a part of His household and the culture of heaven until you smell like the essence of Him who saves and restores you.

How do we do this? By staying in constant connection to Him throughout our day, not just at certain times of the day. We are invited to abide in Him at all times, not only to have devotional times and then go on with our days as if He does not exist. As we keep our affections turned toward Him throughout the day, He takes up residence within us, abiding with us, creating an atmosphere of peace all around us.

This kind of living will not come naturally at first, but it is crucial if we want to grow in His peace and bear fruit for the Kingdom of God. Jesus tells us, "I am the vine; you are the branches. If you remain in me and I in you, you will bear much fruit; apart from me you can do nothing" (John 15:5). If we are to grow in peace, then we must learn to immerse ourselves in Him and abide in Him. Peace can only be cultivated in relationship with Christ.

God has given us a covenant of peace through the Gospel, thus making peace central to the Gospel. Jesus' death and resurrection bring peace to our souls, giving us wholeness and health and deliverance from the effects of the Fall. The Gospel is much more than the assurance of heaven when we die; it changes the very fabric of our lives in the here and now. We have peace with God through our Lord Jesus Christ.

■ **PRAYER FOR PEACE** ■

Father, help me to stay in constant communion with You throughout the day. Help my affections to be turned toward You at all times, causing me to experience Your deep peace that passes all understanding. Thank You for the assurance that I am going to heaven when this life ends, but I also thank You that I can experience so much more of Your peace in this present life. Open my eyes to see all that is contained in the Gospel, giving me peace that brings wholeness to my spirit, soul and body. Thank You for reconciling me to Yourself through Your precious Son. I pray these things in Your name. Amen.

■ 4 ■

Growing in Peace

But the fruit of the Spirit is love, joy, peace, forbearance, kindness, goodness, faithfulness, gentleness and self-control.

Galatians 5:22–23

The peace of God is one of the first fruits of the Spirit we experience and grow in when we access our relationship with Christ. The fruit of peace begins as a tiny bud that must be nurtured by Jesus Christ. As we walk in our relationship with Christ, He nurtures what needs to be grown within us. When we allow peace to grow within us, it becomes a powerful and dominant force in the garden of life that dispels chaos as it spreads to those around us.

Peace is not something that we should hold close, as if it were only for us and the situation we are facing. If we think of the peace that has grown in our lives as part of the larger garden plot in the middle of a community, it is easier to envision the fruits of peace being available to and for the benefit of everyone connected with us. This communal aspect of the fruit of the Spirit is quite biblical.

Giving Peace Away

In the Old Testament, fields of grain were farmed by their owners, but the corners of the fields were left for the poor and the needy to harvest when they had nothing to eat (see Leviticus 23:22). In the same way, your growth in peace is beneficial to you and for the nourishment of your soul in Christ; it also has the ability, however, to benefit others around you who are in need.

Another way to think about this is to see your life as a river, not a pond. A pond lacks movement—water goes in but not out—and, because of this, ponds become stagnant and easily polluted. You may feel like you are getting a lot from your time in church and your Bible reading and prayer times, but if you are not allowing all that is flowing into you to flow out from you, then you will become a stagnant pool.

One of the foundational revelations of the Kingdom of God that needs to be understood is that in order to keep the peace we have received, we must give it away. When I think of the Dead Sea, I cannot help but wonder if God placed it in Israel as a reminder for those in covenant with Him to always release what they have been given so that God's gifts can continue to produce life within them.

Peace manifests when we give it away, not when we retain it. God does not intend for us to be dead seas; we are to be conduits of the water of His Spirit so that we and all those around us will never be dry and thirsty. This is one of the reasons Jesus said, "Let anyone who is thirsty come to me and drink. Whoever believes in me, as Scripture has said, rivers of living water will flow from within them" (John 7:37–38). We have rivers of living water flowing from within us—life-giving peace is continually flowing out of us. It is not dead and stagnant; it is living and continuously gushing out of our innermost being. Peace given away is peace that continues to grow.

Growing in Real-World Peace

When talking with others about the challenges of faithfully living the Christian life, the topic of taking what we receive from God and applying it to everyday life often comes up. It is encouraging to sit in church and hear a message on the peace of God or to curl up in your favorite spot at home with your Bible, but it is another thing altogether to take what you learn into a work environment or a household that is in conflict. Kingdom living in the real world takes discipline.

As a husband, father of small children, a son, a brother and a friend, I am constantly dealing with situations that threaten to derail my peace. I remember so clearly the day I set out to help my parents clean out their house of thirty years in preparation for a move. In the midst of a bruising work schedule, leaving my wife at home with our two-year-old, our one-year-old and our newborn, I set out to meet up with my brother on the way to my parents' house.

A bit on the edge of exhaustion and feeling the weight of life's pressures, I made the decision to worship, talk to Jesus and to turn my affections toward Him as I drove to pick up my brother. It was a glorious morning. I saw the sunrise and wildlife all around. The presence of God filled my car, and my heart felt full. Arriving in the small town where my brother lived, I gave the car a quick wash and even ministered to the car-wash attendant. I was giving away the peace I had in me, and I wanted to keep on giving it away, which is when I began to bump up against resistance to the Kingdom fruit that was flowing out of me.

After picking up my brother, we headed back out on the highway. I was in the left lane going about seventy when my front left tire blew out and the car started to swerve. Instantly, adrenaline shot through my veins. Thankfully, traffic was light because it was early in the day, and I was able to pull over safely. Although I was thankful we were safe, the incident opened up a flood of anxiety. Negative thoughts raced through my mind:

Are we going to be late now?

We don't have time for this.

Of course, something like this is happening now.

As I wrestled with my anxious thoughts, I realized that the shoulder on the side of the road was too small to change the tire safely. More pressure. I called my tow company, but they could not make it. Again, I experienced more pressure. I had to call another tow company, which cost even more money. The pressure was continually building. All I had in the way of a spare was one of those worthless donut tires. Even if the car was towed to a station to change the tire, I would have to buy a new tire. Still more pressure. My pressure tank was so full that it was threatening to spill over and obliterate my peace.

By the time the tire issue was resolved, the day was almost gone. We were hours late getting to my parents' house.

There was not enough time to get everything accomplished and for me to get back home for work the following day. The conflict and the pressure and the chaos left me tempted to become angry and allow the circumstances to affect me. Something within me rose up and I said, "I won't let go of my peace. I won't become a dead sea. What little peace is left within me needs to flow out." Rather than letting the world change me, I determined that I was going to continue to change the world.

We managed to get in some productive hours helping my parents pack up and move, and I made it home safe and sound later that evening. God's peace carried the day.

Becoming a Thermostat

The way I see life, we have two options: We can be either a thermostat or a thermometer. Thermometers tell the temperature and climate of a room, but thermostats actually change the temperature and set the climate of a room. Think of the fruit of peace working in you and through you as something that strengthens your thermostat capabilities— your ability to change an environment. As *thermostats*, we can confront real-life circumstances and choose to express peace until the environment matches what is inside of us.

The world will push back on our peace, like a warm front encountering a cold front. Instability sets up and can result in storms, depending on which front is stronger. Peacemakers step into the midst of instability and release stability in the form of God's peace, because the climate we carry has no end. Sometimes, it is just about recognizing what is really happening in our everyday conflicts and adjusting our thermostat accordingly. This is a discipline that can be learned, and after a while, we can leave our spiritual thermostat set on *auto.*

Jesus said, "Blessed are the peacemakers, for they will be called children of God" (Matthew 5:9). The Greek translation for the word *peacemaker* means "one who produces peace" or "one who makes peaceful."[1] It is impossible to be a peacemaker, at least the way Jesus intended it, without the Prince of Peace taking up residence in our souls. We must stay connected to Jesus and choose to be bold and fearless in peace if we are to grow in peace and strengthen our thermostat capabilities.

Even though we are called to be peacemakers and to grow in the fruit of peace, it can seem like peace is so elusive at times. I was amazed to learn that the U.S. has only been at peace for eight percent of its recorded history. The United States of America has been at war 222 out of 239 years since its independence in 1776. That is less than twenty years, or seven percent of her history, where she has been at peace with other nations and with herself.[2] Peace truly is rare and difficult to attain, which is perhaps why so many beauty pageant contestants wish for world peace. The world is desperate for peace and crying out for peacemakers to rise up and step into their anointing, bringing an end to the chaos and conflict that constantly surround us.

Romans 12:18 says, "If it is possible, as far as it depends on you, live at peace with everyone." It is interesting that Paul does not mention the one we may be tempted to blame in a conflict; instead, Paul focuses on our responsibility regardless of the other person's role in stealing our peace. I love that Paul says, "as far as it depends on you."

The peace that we carry is not dependent on whether or not the other person is also at peace with us; it is only dependent upon our relationship with Jesus, the Prince of Peace, and our obedience to walk with the Holy Spirit in His perfect peace.

The key to this kind of lifestyle—becoming a peace thermostat—is a committed relationship with Jesus Christ that involves daily communion with Him through prayer. When your prayer life slips, so does your peace. It has been my experience that if I want a peaceful home and peaceful children, or peaceful relationships with my family, my friends and my co-workers, then I need to pray for peace, declare peace and seek to walk in peace.

Cultivating a Peaceful Atmosphere

If you want to grow as a person of peace and as a person who changes the atmosphere around you through peace, then start by going back to a place where you encountered God's peace in your own life. There is no better way to gauge how you are growing in peace than to go into places that aren't peaceful and partnering with Jesus to release His peace. For me, that meant going back and ministering in bars.

People who frequent bars typically are not living peace-filled lives. They go into these dark, smoke-filled environments to drown their sorrows and forget about the world. But there are so many people hanging out in bars who never go to church and who will never hear the Gospel. The only way they are going to encounter Jesus is if He sovereignly reveals Himself to them or if someone brings them to an encounter with Jesus. I cannot do anything to make sovereign visitations happen, but I can go into a bar and help others encounter Jesus.

I walked into a local bar that was frequented by students from the nearby college. Hazy smoke filled the air. Off to one side, people played pool. The lighting was just low enough to hide the dirty floors and the walls in need of a fresh coat of paint. I walked up and sat on a stool and ordered my usual virgin drink (you do not need to drink alcohol in a bar). Knowing that people in the bar are willing to talk to you as long as you do not have an agenda, I sipped my drink and talked about normal, everyday things with those around me. People can sense when we have an agenda, but when we are motivated by love, evangelism will naturally happen.

Eventually I struck up a conversation about dating and marriage with a young woman who was nearby. Because people love talking about themselves, if you allow them to open up, opportunities to minister will naturally happen. As this young lady continued to talk to me, she shared about her struggles with an ex-boyfriend.

Even though they were no longer dating, every time he would call, she would end up sleeping with him and hating herself for it. She did not love him anymore and did not want to keep giving herself away, but she could not seem to stop. I explained the meaning of soul ties and how, when we have sex with someone, it is much more than a physical exchange taking place. Emotional and spiritual ties are made, which is why it can be so hard to break those ungodly bonds.

I could see that she was becoming receptive to what God had for her, so I asked if I could pray for her. With her permission, I took her hand and quietly began to pray for Jesus to break the soul ties in her life and give her His peace. Evangelism in the real world does not have to be over the top. For all outward appearances, we were just two people sitting at a bar holding hands. As I prayed, tears began to roll down her cheeks. It was such a peaceful but powerful God encounter.

The girl on the other side of me was watching the whole time and knew something special was taking place. Before long, she was talking to me about her father who had left her and how hard life had been without him. I shared how God, our heavenly Father, will never leave us or forsake us. Then I prayed with her, asking for God's peace to flood her soul. Tears began to stream down her cheeks as God's love and peace touched her heart. When the bartender noticed the two girls on either side of me crying, he asked what was going on. At that moment, I got a word of knowledge that his tooth was bad and causing him a lot of pain. He allowed me to pray for him and was instantly healed.

As the bartender was getting healed, a woman came up to get her drink refilled, noticed something extraordinary was going on and wanted in. Excited, the bartender started talking about how God had touched these two ladies and healed his tooth. Emboldened by the testimonies, she showed me a soft cast on her arm from carpal tunnel surgery and said she was in a lot of pain. With her drink still in her hand, she let me pray for her. By this time, a small crowd had formed around us. After we prayed, she took off her cast, moved her arm around and then screamed, "I'm healed!" Everyone in the bar cheered.

This dark place was filled with the peace and atmosphere of heaven. The two ladies whose hearts were healed accepted Christ that night. And it all happened because I chose to be a peacemaker—I chose to let the peace in me conquer the darkness around me.

A peacemaker is someone who works to bring the climate of heaven to overpower every situation dwelling in the chaos of darkness, who fights for the reconciliation of children to their Father God, thereby triumphing over the kingdom of darkness. When we look at the Scriptures, we see Jesus embodying the true peacemaker who constantly brought people into reconciliation with His Father in heaven. When two kingdoms collide—the Kingdom of God and the kingdom of darkness—as they did in the bar that night—there can only be one victor, and His name is Jesus Christ.

▪ PRAYER FOR PEACE ▪

Jesus, I want to live as a peacemaker in this chaotic world. Help me to embody Your peace. Teach me to be a thermostat, setting the temperature of Your peace for all those around me. Help me not to react to what is taking place around me, but to be a peacemaker who is influencing and giving away the peace You have given to me. I do not want peace just for myself, but to give it away to others. God, help peace to fill my soul each day, and help me grow in the fruit of peace. I want to experience Your rivers of living water flowing out of me. Help me give away peace to all I encounter today. In Your name, I pray. Amen.

◾ 5 ◾

Living as Peacemakers

"Blessed are the peacemakers, for they will be called children of God."

Matthew 5:9

By nature, humanity has been hostile toward God since the Fall of Adam and Eve in the Garden of Eden. Paul writes about some of the effects of the Fall in Romans 8:7–8 (TPT): "In fact, the mind-set focused on the flesh fights God's plan and refuses to submit to his direction, because it cannot! For no matter how hard they try, God finds no pleasure with those who are controlled by the flesh." Humanity, without knowing God, hates Him, not because we know Him and have chosen to abandon Him, but because we do not want to know Him or acknowledge His existence.

Often, salvation is not a matter of looking at evidence and choosing to believe in the One who gave His life for us, but rather acknowledging the possibility of a loving and eternal God. When we are bound in sin, we are separated from God and from the true knowledge of Him. But thank God for His Son, Jesus Christ, who paid the penalty of death for our sins so that we could overcome our flesh and be empowered by the Spirit to believe in Jesus Christ, thus having peace with our Father in heaven.

Paul continues:

> But when the Spirit of Christ empowers your life, you are not dominated by the flesh but by the Spirit. And if you are not joined to the Spirit of the Anointed One, you are not of him. Now Christ lives his life in you! And even though your body may be dead because of the effects of sin, His life-giving Spirit imparts life to you because you are fully accepted by God.
>
> Romans 8:9–10 TPT

At the cross, Jesus bore our sins, which was the ultimate price of reconciliation with God the Father, what Paul calls being "fully accepted by God." Jesus brought peace to humanity by bearing our iniquities on the cross and paying the price for our sins; we no longer have to be "dominated by the flesh but by the Spirit." Jesus is the ultimate peacemaker because He made reconciliation with God the Father possible for all of humanity. Paul confirms this when he writes:

> Therefore, if anyone is in Christ, the new creation has come: The old has gone, the new is here! All this is from God, who reconciled us to himself through Christ and gave us the ministry of reconciliation: that God was recon-

ciling the world to himself in Christ, not counting people's sins against them. And he has committed to us the message of reconciliation. . . . God made him who had no sin to be sin for us, so that in him we might become the righteousness of God.

2 Corinthians 5:17–19, 21

Beyond the removal of our sins, Jesus also visibly displayed on earth what being a peacemaker looked like in a person's life.

The Ultimate Peacemaker

When Jesus ministered to the woman at the well, for example, He broke down the barriers of race and class and gender, thus showing Himself to be the ultimate peacemaker. John writes about this encounter in his gospel: "The Samaritan woman said to him, 'You are a Jew and I am a Samaritan woman. How can you ask me for a drink?' (For Jews do not associate with Samaritans)" (John 4:9).

In Jesus' day, Samaritans were considered half-breeds (i.e., half-Jews and half-Gentiles) who were despised by the Jewish people. Centuries of opposition between the Jews and the Samaritans went back to Israel's division into two kingdoms—Israel and Judah—and the disdain the Jews felt with the mixed marriages and worship that took place between their northern cousins and the Assyrians, dating some 550 years previous (see 2 Kings 17). Walls of bitterness had grown between the two sides, which did nothing but harden over time, and which were clearly seen in Jesus' day.

In Luke 9:51–53, the Samaritans rejected Jesus when He passed through Samaria while on His way to Jerusalem. Part of this rejection stemmed from the Jewish belief that the correct place to worship God was in Jerusalem, whereas Samaritans believed it was on a mountain in Samaria. This is evident in John 4:20, where the Samaritan woman said to Jesus, "Our ancestors worshiped on this mountain, but you Jews claim that the place where we must worship is in Jerusalem."

Jesus reconciled this divide and responded by saying, "Woman, . . . believe me, a time is coming when you will worship the Father neither on this mountain nor in Jerusalem. You Samaritans worship what you do not know; we worship what we do know, for salvation is from the Jews" (John 4:21–22).

Jesus, our ultimate peacemaker, through His simple yet profound actions at the well, broke down the barriers between race, class, gender and religion and ministered to this woman's heart. Consequently, the Samaritan woman eagerly drank from the living water of eternal life that Jesus spoke to her about and became an evangelist to her own town. Now, that is true peacemaking at the highest level.

Another less obvious example of Jesus as a peacemaker is found in Matthew 21. Jesus went into the Temple and drove out the merchants and money changers while boldly declaring, "It is written, . . . 'My house will be called a house of prayer,' but you are making it a 'den of robbers'" (Matthew 21:12–13). This was not a passive moment for Jesus. He rose up in righteous anger, furious that God's house was being corrupted and turned into a place that took advantage of the poor and the widowed rather than fulfilling its purpose as a place of worship. Jesus was not afraid to act and speak boldly. He demanded justice for the marginalized and, as such, was considered a rebel and a troublemaker by the law-abiding religious people of the day.

This was the Temple that was considered to be the one and only place where God's presence dwelt among His people. Each year, during Passover, faithful Jews came from all over Israel to the Temple to celebrate God's protection over His people. Estimates tell us that there were between three and four hundred thousand people at the Temple during Passover.[1] Each person was required to pay a fee just to enter the Temple, and once inside, a sacrificial animal was purchased to present to the priest in order to be purified so that person could worship God. The wealthy could afford to purchase large animals, while women, the poor and other outcasts could only afford to purchase doves for their sacrifices.

Seeing this corruption in His Father's house, Jesus was moved to action. His actions and teachings outraged the religious authorities, threatening the profitable and powerful positions they held. It was this response of anger, which was fueled by fear, that caused the religious leaders of the day to plot to kill Jesus (see Mark 11:18).

Bringing God's reign of peace requires the boldness of Jesus, not in physically violent actions, but with a violently passionate heart that longs to see His Kingdom come on the earth just as it is in heaven. This is what being a peacemaker is all about—bringing the peace of heaven to bear on our current situations or circumstances. Jesus said, "Blessed are the peacemakers, for they will be called children of God" (Matthew 5:9).

Blessed Are the Peacemakers

What does it look like to be a peacemaker? First, it is important to understand that peacemaking is not synonymous with pacifism or passivity. God's peacemakers work to bring conflict to an end, not to shut their mouths while injustice runs rampant all around them. Jesus, the ultimate peacemaker, gave us the gift of God's peace through the most violent way imaginable—a brutal death by crucifixion. Real peace does not ignore conflict; rather, peacemakers invoke action in the midst of conflict.

The Greek word used for *peacemaker* is *eirēnopoiós*, which means "one who produces peace" or "one who makes peaceful."[2] *Eirēnopoiós* is a compound word, which is made up of two words—a noun, *eirēnē*, and a verb, *poieō*. *Eirēnē* means "freedom from fear," "exemption from the rage and havoc of war," "harmony between individuals" and "a treaty of peace between countries."[3] The last part of the word, *poieō*, is an action word, which means "to make, to produce, to be the author of, to create, to bring forth, to render, to cause one to, to perform, to make ready, and to do."[4] Taken altogether, peacemaking is a word exploding with energy. It demands action and initiative.

To be a peacemaker, then, we do not only talk of peace or dream of peace or hope for peace. No, we get up and do something to bring about peace and to put an end to the conflict and chaos reigning over a specific situation, because *He* who is in us is greater than any place of darkness or fear.

Although some people may have a specific mantle or anointing for peacemaking, every single Christian is called to be a peacemaker. Just as we are all called to spread the Gospel and to heal the sick, so we all have the ministry of peace too. When we lead someone to salvation, we bring about an end to the spiritual conflict in that person's life. When we pray for someone and see that person healed from pain and disease, we see the peace of God taking control of that individual's situation. The Kingdom of God is the Kingdom of peace, and we are all, as children of God, called to bring the Kingdom of God to the earth. We are invited to access and release God's peace.

Striving to Create Peace

Lest we are mistaken, peacemaking is not the same thing as peacekeeping. In fact, peacemaking is the opposite of peacekeeping. Peacekeepers strive to keep peace by avoiding conflict; they do whatever it takes to keep peace at all costs. Peacemakers, on the other hand, strive to create peace, even if that means disturbing false peace in an attempt to reconcile what is at odds. In biblical times, peacemakers were people of influence who could enforce or bring about peace in a given situation.

The apostle Paul is a great example of this. In Paul's short letter to Philemon, he contends for peace between Philemon, a slave owner, and his runaway slave, Onesimus. Paul writes, "So if you consider me a partner, welcome [Onesimus] as you would welcome me. If he has done you any wrong or owes you anything, charge it to me" (Philemon 17–18). Again, in Acts 15, Paul and Barnabas create peace within the Church between the Jewish Christians and the Gentile Christians over the matter of circumcision.

Being a peacemaker does not mean that people will never get upset with what we do or what we say. Jesus greatly upset the Pharisees when He went about healing the sick and spreading the Gospel of peace. As children of God, we bring the Kingdom of peace into specific situations, not from a worldly position where peace is brought about through our own strength and our own striving, but as Kingdom peacemakers through the power of peace that is only found in Jesus.

Jesus told His disciples, "Peace I leave with you, my peace I give unto you: not as the world giveth, give I unto you. Let not your heart be troubled, neither let it be afraid" (John 14:27 KJV). I love the Greek alternative translation to this verse: "A time of peace I let go to you. My tranquility I hand over to you. But not how a worldly power grants it. I appoint you as priests. Do not let your feelings bother you. Do not be afraid."[5]

Jesus was passing His peace on to us, His disciples, thus appointing us to continue His work of bringing peace to the people we encounter. It is not a peace that is conjured up or forced out of human will, but a peace that is filled with the supernatural power of heaven to overpower and reign over every situation of chaos and fear in the world. It is an all-empowering, all-consuming, overwhelming peace that not only calms our internal chaos but also has the power to destroy the chaos over our current circumstances, as well as the chaos in our cities, our nation and beyond.

Peace in Chaotic Situations

A number of years ago, I took a team to minister in a small African country that was recovering from civil war. There was much corruption, and it was not an easy place to visit. We had come to minister and to donate new clothing to the poor children there. When our plane landed, I began to take the clothing and gear out of the airport to the shuttles that were waiting for us. I was the first one through the immigration line, so I was by myself and trying to get a lot done for the team so we could be on our way once they came through immigration.

At one point, a large man dressed in full military regalia came over to me with a machine gun and ushered me into a retaining room inside the airport. With his weapon pointed at my back, he began yelling at me, but I did not hear anything he was saying. Fear came upon my body. I froze. My heart rate rose through the roof, and my mind began to race with scenarios of never being seen again. He finally stopped yelling and left the room, locking the door behind him.

As I stood there in that locked room with the realization that I could be beaten, or worse, and no one on my team would ever know, a simple thought came to me: *What is fear going to do compared to peace?* At that moment, I had a choice. I could stay in fear knowing that it would breed more fear, or I could turn my affections toward the Prince of Peace and walk in that peace and everything that comes with it. As I turned my heart toward Him, a strong weight of God's peace immediately came upon me. Fear drained from my body, and my mind cleared. I started knocking on the door and would not stop.

After a few minutes, the soldier came back and opened the door. When he did, I looked him in the eyes and calmly but boldly told him he was mistaken, that whatever his issue was, it was not with me, and it was wrong for him to walk me in that room at gunpoint. At first, he seemed annoyed until I started to explain why we were there and that we were on our way to meet with children at a poor school where we would give them the clothes we brought with us. As I talked with him, his countenance changed, and he apologized and let me go. Just like that, I quickly walked to the shuttles, and the team and I left for our destination.

John 8:36 tells us, "So if the Son sets you free, you will be free indeed." We can be slaves to fear while living outside the family of God, or we can receive our inheritance as sons and daughters of God and walk in the freedom of His peace. I chose to access and release the peace of God that day, even though my initial response was fear. As peacemakers, we have the ability to access the supernatural power of peace and release that peace to overpower the chaos and fear that are trying to overwhelm us. It was God's peace that destroyed the chaos over that situation, changing the soldier's countenance and allowing me to go on my way with the rest of the team.

Cultivating a Culture of Peace

My amazing wife, Ruth, knows firsthand what it is like to be surrounded by chaos and the challenge to peace that comes with day-to-day life. She is a stay-at-home mother of our three children, ages three, two and one, with one more on the way. And, yes, we actually wanted it this way. In our house there are often days when peace seems as far out of reach as the moon. Truly we have our hands full, yet we actually believe it is more like we have our arms full to overflowing.

There is so much beauty found in the whirlwind of raising multiple children who are close in age. In the midst of the beautiful craziness of it all, the greatest revelation that Ruth discovered as a mother is that if she wants peace in the home, then she has to be the one who brings it. There are opportunities for being the peacemaker and reconciling one toddler to another or one child to a parent too many times in a day. But if Ruth and I are ever not at peace when these situations arise, and if we do not respond out of a place of peace, then more often than not neither do the children.

Like most families, when it comes to reconciliation, chaos and fear often ensue rather than peace and love (albeit with correction and discipline). Children are clever little beings who pick up on the atmosphere around them and, without hesitation, seem to jump right in, whether good or bad. We have learned the hard way that no matter how frustrating, disobedient, disrespectful, angry or even violent a child is, the best response toward him or her, even in disciplining that child, is from a place of peace. In the face of peace, chaos flees.

Despite our best efforts, our children, in their free will, may not always respond as peacefully as we hope. Despite all the challenges, we believe in cultivating a culture of peace in our home so that, over time, our children will absorb peace into every part of their being until it works its way into their souls and they become little agents of peace themselves. We have to represent peace in every situation if we want to have peace in every situation.

No matter where we are—at home, work or a store—we can bring God's peace to bear on that situation. Sometimes this is as easy as walking in the anointing of peace we have been given as children of God, but at other times it is about choosing peace as our response, even when it feels completely unnatural and difficult. Peacemakers cultivate a culture of peace.

Confronting Injustice

Peacemakers are also evangelists, which means they confront nonbelievers with the Gospel in order to bring them to salvation. It is all well and good to sit quietly and peacefully in the comfort and safety of our church pews. We do need times of corporate worship and fellowship—those are vital to our growth in godliness. There is a time to sit and learn, but there is also a time to get up and go with the Gospel, confronting the social evils and injustices we see in the world. God will use us to change history in the smallest of ways, but sometimes He may even do it in big ways.

Martin Luther King Jr. is a great example of a peacemaker and an evangelist who was used by God to change history in a big way. As a Bible-believing Christian, Dr. King used biblical wisdom coupled with sociopolitical knowledge to confront the evil injustice of racial segregation in the United States, becoming one of the most prominent voices in the fight for civil rights. The world is begging for peacemakers who will step out and confront evil.

Like other civil rights activists of his day, Dr. King had to disturb the peace in order to make room for true peace. He did this through his ability to love others and the pursuit of change through nonviolence and civil disobedience. In his sermon "Loving Your Enemies," Dr. King points to Jesus and the Sermon on the Mount as an example of being a loving peacemaker while confronting social evil. Jesus said, "You have heard that it was said, 'Love your neighbor and hate your enemy.' But I tell you, love your enemies and pray for those who persecute you, that you may be children of your Father in heaven" (Matthew 5:43–45). King's teaching on the necessity of love is one of my favorites: "But far from being an impractical idealist, Jesus has become the practical realist. . . . Far from being the pious injunction of a utopian dreamer, this command [to love your enemies] is an absolute necessity for the survival of our civilization. Yes, it is love that will save our world and our civilization, love even for enemies."[6]

Loving our enemies does not mean that we agree with them or even like them or what they stand for. God's love is bigger than our human parameters; it calls us to a much higher place. Walking in love and being a person of love are the foundational core of a peacemaker. Dr. King put it this way: "Love is . . . the refusal to defeat any individual. When you rise to the level of love, of its great beauty and power, you seek only to defeat evil systems. Individuals who happen to be caught up in that system, you love, but you seek to defeat the system."[7]

As Dr. King so visibly demonstrated, revolution only happens when we work to end violence through acts of nonviolence and love. It is about forgiveness at all costs and loving our enemies even when we hate the offense. To bring about true and lasting change in this world, we sometimes have to be the person who gets our hands dirty or the person who forgives the oppressor and creates peace through love. If there are any areas of injustice you see in the world today, then ask yourself, "What can I do about this?" Be the change you want to see in the world by accessing and releasing God's peace. That is the mission of the peacemaker.

▪ PRAYER FOR PEACE ▪

God, I pray that boldness and wisdom will increase in my heart, that Your peace will strengthen within me and overflow out of me into all areas of my life. I pray that there would be open doors and divine appointments for me to be a peacemaker in the spheres of influence You have given to me. May I be known in my region as a peacemaker to reconcile God with the world as well as people with other people. Help me to rise up in my authority to which You have called me as a peacemaker and have the boldness to release peace in all circumstances of my life. In the name of Your precious Son, I pray. Amen.

■ 6 ■

Advancing in Peace

And having shod your feet with the preparation of
the gospel of peace . . .

Ephesians 6:15 NKJV

We often think of peace as stillness and that what is at
peace is at rest. That is to say, we are most at peace when
our house is the quietest, when our minds are still and
when we do not think about all of the things we have to
do for that day. In the Kingdom of heaven, however, this
is not true peace. Rather, biblical peace is advancement.
It is forward movement. It is not sitting still and becoming mindful; it is forcefully advancing the Gospel by our
actions and our words.

In the book of Ephesians, the apostle Paul gives us a
way to appropriate God's peace at all times and in every
situation. Ephesians 6 is the well-known "armor of God"
passage. Those of you who grew up in church know it

well because you, like me, may have been subjected to the plastic armor-of-God demonstration at some point in your Sunday school experience. The demonstration would go something like this: Someone would stand up and put on the plastic pieces of armor, one piece at a time, as the teacher explained the significance of each piece. "Now, children," the teacher would say, "this is the helmet of salvation that protects your mind in Christ. This is the sword of the Spirit, which is the Word of God. This is the breastplate of righteousness that protects you from evil, and here is the belt of truth that goes around your waist. And here is the shield of faith that will extinguish all the fiery darts of the evil one."

As a kid, I always thought it was funny that the shoes of peace got the least emphasis, as if the apostle Paul did not quite know what to say about them. Did he run out of body parts by the time he got to peace, so he just put it on the feet? All kidding aside, I do not think it is a coincidence that peace ended up on the feet. No matter how well we hold our shield or wave our sword, if we do not have God's peace, then we are not going anywhere. We only advance by moving forward. Likewise, the Kingdom of heaven only advances on the forward movement of the peace of God.

Walking in the Peace of God

The city of Harrisburg is the state capital of Pennsylvania. The 2008 recession hit Harrisburg hard. They were already over budget (in large part due to a foolish investment in a revamp of its incinerator), so not long after the recession came, they were the first capital in the United States to attempt to file for bankruptcy.[1]

One of the effects of the recession was that as the level of poverty rose within the city, the value placed on life declined. When we would go out on the streets to evangelize in Harrisburg, some of our people ended up beaten and sent to the hospital. We quickly learned not to bring our wallets when we witnessed and shared the love of God. In fact, the situation became so severe that the city stationed police officers on the corners next to the schools because children were being assaulted and robbed of their lunch money by twenty-year-old men. A taxi driver was shot in the back of the head over a small taxi fare.[2] Unspeakable violence is a result of great poverty.

A friend of mine named Jen had a house bought for her to manage in one of the poorest and most dangerous areas in the city. The heart of both the buyer of the house and Jen were positioned to bring the love of Jesus to those who were hardest hit by both the recession and life in general. The houses in that area at the time were worth less than the average price of a new car. And so, with help, Jen fixed up the house and invited students from a nearby ministry school to rent rooms from her. These were all young women. In the natural, it was not a sensible thing to do, but they heard the call of God and were obedient to what He had placed in their hearts. Part of their heavenly assignment was to love the women and children who lived nearby, and to help those who were battling alcohol addiction get into rehab.

Jen and the other young women carried an amazing love for the city and its people. They refused to take even the simplest safety measures for their home, such as putting bars over the windows or installing a home security system. They did not even get a guard dog; they got a kitten instead. From time to time, I would get a call from Jen telling me that someone had broken in and stolen their copper pipes again. Refusing to lock themselves away from the community, Jen and her roommates would replace what had been stolen and continue to shine a light in the neighborhood.

One day, Mary—one of the girls living in the house—was walking home in broad daylight from the corner convenience store. A man suddenly jumped out of the alley and put a knife to her throat. "If you move or scream," he said, "I'm going to kill you."

Most of us would respond to that kind of a situation with a whole range of negative emotions, such as fright, flight or fear. Not Mary. She simply looked the man straight in the eyes and said, "Can I tell you about Jesus?"

The guy paused for a moment and then took off running in the other direction. Was this the end of the story? Nope. Mary started running after him, yelling, "Wait, wait!" She truly just wanted to tell him about Jesus. It was as if the man with the knife was the embodiment of fear and Mary was a representation of the peace of God. In the presence of God's peace, fear has no choice but to flee.

Peace Destroys the Authority of Chaos

The ancient Hebrew alphabet is more than just phonetic letters; the Hebrew language is pictorial. Like in all languages, words evolve over time, so the etymology of a word will often be lost when it enters into modern talk. For example, the word *awful* used to mean worthy of awe, but it has a totally different meaning now, such as something tasting horrible. Likewise, the word *awesome* is meant to capture the way we feel standing at the edge of something magnificent, such as the Grand Canyon, but nowadays we hear the word *awesome* used to describe a taco. When we understand the original meaning of a word in its root language, then we gain new levels of insight that have the ability to reveal the power of that word.

Consider the word *shalom.* Although it has retained much of its original depth and meaning, it is now frequently used to greet a person. But when we study this word in the Hebrew language, we see that it is made up of four letters that represent four pictures. The first letter (from right to left) is a picture of teeth that resemble our letter W, but it means "to destroy." The second letter looks like a shepherd's staff, and it means "authority." The third letter looks like a nail and is considered an attaching letter, while the fourth letter is a picture of crashing waves of water associated with chaos. When we put all of the letters together, we see God's definition of peace, which is "to destroy the authority that is attached to chaos."[3] Now, that is powerful indeed.

When we speak *shalom* over somebody or even over our own circumstances, we are declaring that the authority that is attached to the chaos is destroyed as we come in the name of Jesus. Whatever problem we think we are facing is not really the problem at all; it is merely a symptom of a greater issue. Chaos is merely a manifestation of the authority that rules over the chaos. If we are dealing with a demonic attack, for instance, when we speak peace over that situation, we are commanding the demonic authority to be destroyed, thus bringing an end to the chaos. Peace destroys the authority that is attached to chaos.

I was speaking on the power of peace when a young man came forward to receive prayer. He was dressed in dark clothes with long hair that covered his eyes. As he stood before me, he looked sheepish with his head bowed down to the ground. It was obvious that he was not familiar or comfortable with coming to someone for prayer. But overcome by the presence of God, he began to cry. So, I lightly placed my hand on his shoulder and began to bless him with the peace of God, repeating these words: "I bless you with real peace. I bless you with His peace." Tears streamed down his face as God touched his hurting heart, and he fell down under the presence of the Spirit.

Robert later told me that he had never experienced anything like that before. He felt like a band that was around his head snapped, and the darkness and depression that had been his constant companions broke off him that evening. Demonic depression had repeatedly brought him to the brink of suicide, robbing him of healing and wholeness. He would sometimes hurt himself out of self-hatred. The weight of God's peace crushed the demonic stronghold on this young man's life. He gave his life to Jesus that night. A few weeks later, he wrote me to tell me that he was at peace for the first time and had applied to community college. Not long after that, he got a job and began to live a normal life.

Releasing God's Peace into Brokenness

It is important to note that not all chaos is demonic. Much of the chaos we find ourselves in is a result of the sin of our broken world. When we speak God's peace into sinful, broken situations, that peace breaks the authority of sin over the situation so that God's Kingdom peace can reign. When we declare peace over a person who is sick and in need of healing, that Kingdom peace breaks the authority over the sickness and disease, bringing wholeness and health from God. In fact, God's peace has so much gravitas that, when we speak it, we should feel the weight of the word because all of heaven is backing it up.

Since Randy does not like to waste time while we are on the road, we are typically in meetings from the time we land until the time we leave. It is a physically taxing schedule, but I am appreciative that he has trained me in this way. It is a pace that allows him to maximize his time for the Lord while also making time for family at home.

Randy preached the first night of a conference, just a few hours after our plane landed, and prayed for the sick afterward. Around eleven o'clock that night, I could see that he needed to get back to the hotel to rest because he was so tired from the flight and ministering to the sick. Going over to the line of people still waiting to receive prayer, I told them Randy would be leaving in a few minutes, but he would be back the following day. I reminded them that if they did not want to wait until the next day to receive prayer, there was a ministry team that would love to pray for them that evening.

One of the women in line became distraught and was not accommodating. She showed her dissatisfaction as she stormed off. Knowing that we cannot please everyone, Randy and I left to go back to the hotel for a much-needed night's rest.

The woman who had been upset the night before returned the next morning, expecting to receive prayer from Randy, only to find me instead. She was again quite upset but remained to hear my talk. As I spoke on the power of peace, God began to speak to her. This dear woman struggled with Asperger syndrome and had no peace in her life. Two of her specific challenges were being in a loud environment and being in public places. The message of peace was just what she needed to hear.

She later told me that from the time she was twelve, she had had thousands of seizures that were misdiagnosed. While in her thirties, she was pretty much bedridden and did not go out much. She was not sure she would even make it to forty. When she would go for a walk, her brain would overload, and she would lose fine-motor skills on her right side, causing her to walk like she had had a stroke. She said that she could not stand worship music and that screams and loud noises sapped her energy for a few days at a time. It made more sense why she had been so upset that night.

God touched her powerfully throughout the service while I was preaching. She came to the front for prayer afterward. I looked her in the eyes and banned confusion, speaking the peace of heaven over her. She received God's peace that day, and her life has never been the same. She told me nearly a year later that the very next day, she went for a five-kilometer walk and did not miss a beat. She no longer has to worry about loud noises or sounds. She can finally be social. She said to me, "Life was like walking on a tightrope with a balance pole. I don't have to do that anymore."

Advancing Kingdom Peace

In the gospel of Mark, Jesus released peace over a storm that threatened His safety and that of His disciples who were in the boat with Him while they were trying to get to the other side of a lake safely (see Mark 4:35–41). As He released His peace and calmed the wind and the waves, He understood that there was no real threat. Arriving at the shore on the other side of the lake, Jesus and His disciples were greeted by a severely demonized man who had been terrorizing the town. So horrible was his behavior that the people of the town kept tying him up and throwing him in a cave, where they hoped he would stay (see Mark 5:1–15).

Mark tells us that the demons were so strong that this man always managed to break the chains and continued to terrorize the town. Everyone lived in fear of him. Everyone but Jesus, that is. When Jesus encountered this man, He cast the demons out of him and drove them into a nearby herd of pigs that were feeding. One would think that the townspeople would be overjoyed to see this man healed, sitting and talking with Jesus, clothed and in his right mind. Wrong. The people were terrified at his new appearance and angry because the demons caused their valuable herd of pigs to run off the edge of a cliff.

There are two things that are important to note about this story. First, Jesus encountered this man and did not yell at him or condemn him. He understood that the man was not the issue here. The issue was the authority that was creating the chaos that was pushing the man around. As soon as Jesus came on the scene, He established who was really in authority and cast the demons out of the man. When Jesus took authority, the enemy was terrified, which is the second point I want to make. When we are at peace, it terrifies the enemy. We do not have to run or live in fear when we are confronted with extremely chaotic situations. All we have to do is appropriate the peace of Jesus that destroys authority over chaos. The key to advancing the Kingdom of God is moving and connecting with the peace of Jesus.

The Roman Empire, with all its brutality and worldly authority, was the context in which Jesus lived and operated. This period of the Roman government is known as the Pax Romana, or the time of Roman peace. [4] It was considered the greatest time of peace for the Roman Empire. The peace that was established and that allowed Rome to rule, however, was due to their conquest of all the nations around them. Kingdom after kingdom fell to the mighty force of Roman power and might. Pax Romana was actually not peaceful at all; it was the subjugation of the weak by the strong. It was into this environment that Jesus brought the peace of God.

The inbreaking of the Kingdom of God that came with the Advent of Jesus Christ brought absolute victory over the enemies of God. This is the kind of authority that Jesus understood and walked in. Demons fled, sickness gave way to health, the lame walked, the blind received their sight and the dead were raised back to life. The Kingdom of God came to the world through the Prince of Peace. But Jesus said He did not come to bring peace, but a sword (see Matthew 10:34–36).

When Jesus instructed His disciples to go into a city and bring peace, He was actually telling them to take God's peace and destroy the supernatural strongholds of that city so that the people could experience God's wholeness and live under His rule instead of the rule of the enemy. His longing is that His Kingdom would come on earth as it is in heaven, and a large part of that Kingdom reign is the inbreaking of His peace. He continues to instruct believers to do the same today. We have been empowered to walk in Kingdom peace, advancing with the Gospel of Jesus Christ by breaking the authority over chaos and bringing God's peace to bear on every situation we face. Our feet have been equipped "with the preparation of the gospel of peace" (Ephesians 6:15 NKJV).

Take a few moments today to pray this prayer to receive His authority and His peace.

▪ PRAYER FOR PEACE ▪

Dear God, I thank You for Your peace that is powerful to destroy the authority that is attached to chaos. Commission me through the power of Your Spirit to go and destroy the works of the enemy and to advance Your Kingdom with the peace of heaven. May all strongholds in every city I enter bow down to the Kingdom of God, and may the shalom of heaven bring every ruler under the authority of the Gospel of Jesus Christ. May I always have my feet shod with the Gospel of peace, to enter homes, businesses, cities and governments with Your peace. In Jesus' name, I pray. Amen.

■ 7 ■

Missional Peace

Therefore, if anyone is in Christ, the new creation has come: The old has gone, the new is here! All this is from God, who reconciled us to himself through Christ and gave us the ministry of reconciliation: that God was reconciling the world to himself in Christ, not counting people's sins against them. And he has committed to us the message of reconciliation.

2 Corinthians 5:17–19

Each of us is called to go and share our story—to tell our testimony and advance the Kingdom of God. Yet, as most believers know, going is not easy, especially when the enemy throws roadblocks in our path, such as fear. It is hard to move forward when we are fearful. That is why Paul exhorts us to be strong, not in our own strength, but in the strength of God's might that enables us to stand in

His peace, and after we have done everything, we are to remain standing. We remove fear from our feet and replace it with the Gospel of peace, so that the anointing of peace propels us to the lost and broken.

Peace is the conduit for the power of God's love to flow through us, and we are like extension cords from heaven to earth. It is never me who heals someone; rather, it is God flowing through me who heals people, much like electricity flowing through an extension cord. Although my cord may become frayed from time to time when I accept fear instead of standing on God's peace, the fact remains that God never changes. His peace is always available to us in every situation that we may face. When we have His peace, His power can flow freely through us.

Peace and Power

In John 14, Jesus was talking to His disciples, preparing them for His crucifixion that was soon to come. He talked of discipling nations, instructing His followers to wait for the precious gift of the Holy Spirit that was promised to them. He said, "But the Helper, the Holy Spirit, whom the Father will send in My name, He will teach you all things, and bring to your remembrance all things that I said to you" (John 14:26 NKJV). Then Jesus said something important that tends to get overlooked:

> Peace I leave with you, My peace I give to you; not as the world gives do I give to you. Let not your heart be troubled, neither let it be afraid.
>
> John 14:27 NKJV

86

In this one statement, Jesus makes a deposit in the disciples, giving them something they cannot have outside of Him. It is a supernatural deposit from heaven to earth, a transference of anointing from His life to theirs. These life-giving words were a powerful and active decree over the lives of His friends and followers. As He spoke, there was a manifestation of God's presence in the actual words. Where there had been no peace moments before, now God's peace rested upon them, readily accessible. Jesus is still giving His peace away to us today. We have the same access that the disciples had nearly two thousand years ago. All we have to do is receive it and tap into it.

In Matthew, Mark and Luke, Jesus instructed His disciples on how to handle the great gift of peace that was theirs to receive (see Matthew 10:5–10; Mark 6:7–13; Luke 9:1–6). In these passages, we find Jesus sending out the disciples to the lost sheep of Israel with instructions to give away what they had freely received—namely, His peace. Notice how transferable this blessing of peace is. Jesus said:

> "As you go, proclaim this message: 'The kingdom of heaven has come near.' Heal the sick, raise the dead, cleanse those who have leprosy, drive out demons. Freely you have received; freely give. . . . As you enter the home, give it your greeting. If the home is deserving, let your peace rest on it; if it is not, let your peace return to you."
>
> Matthew 10:7–8, 12–13

There is a correlation that Jesus makes with bringing healing and bringing peace to a geographical area.

The strongest gift in my life is the gift of healing, but that healing only flows from a place of peace. If you can recognize the call on your life to pray for the sick from a place of peace, then Jesus' power will flow freely through you.

Jesus told His disciples, "Freely you have received; freely give." He is specifically talking about the peace that was given to the disciples so they could freely give it to others. Surely not all disciples were sick or demonized, but they all were given peace through Jesus Christ. And as they received that peace, they were called to release it to others. The sick and the demonized are included in the commission of peace, which is why we need to recognize that bringing peace incorporates the healing and deliverance ministries. Thinking that we can move in peace and not minister to the sick or broken is naïve. Jesus commanded us to move in miracles and healing so that people can experience the Kingdom of heaven firsthand.

A pastor in Brazil, Pastor Danielo, read the gospels and thought, *What a great idea. Let's send our congregation out two by two and knock on every door in town.* He did this with the expectation that they would find at least one house of peace in the city. He assembled his teams, and they went, knocking on doors and asking if anyone in the house needed prayer or a prophetic word or even practical help for their family. The families that responded positively got saved and went on to become lighthouses of peace in the town. They formed home groups and began to minister in their neighborhoods. Pastor Danielo's congregation more than doubled in the first year and has since grown to about ten thousand people.

There are cities all over the world waiting for you—the peacemakers of God—to come and knock on their doors. You are the answer to someone's prayer, because you carry the ultimate peace that fills every void. What the early disciples did, you can also do. Take the combination of peace and power, go out and watch God's blessings change towns, cities and nations.

Peace: A Powerful Weapon

After His death and resurrection, Jesus appeared several times among His disciples. In Luke 24:36, for example, His first words were, "Peace be with you." There were two things going on as He spoke these words to His people. Obviously, the disciples were frightened and confused to have Jesus, who had just suffered and died a gruesome crucifixion, suddenly stand in the midst of them. They were huddled in a locked room. If I had been in that room that day, I would have desperately needed a fresh release of God's peace too. Jesus was releasing His peace over those He loved because, in that moment, they needed it. But He was doing something much more than just a momentary act of kindness.

As a fruit of the Spirit, God's peace has a gentle aspect to it, but it is also a powerful weapon in spiritual warfare. Romans 16:20 reminds us, "The God of peace will soon crush Satan under your feet." Remember that it does not say the God of power will soon crush Satan, although God is all-powerful. It does not say that the God of love will soon crush Satan under your feet, though God is love. The Scripture says it is the God of peace who crushes Satan under our feet.

God's peace is a weapon with great power to disarm our adversary, Satan. With it, we can stand in the darkest of places unaffected by what the enemy brings against us. The devil knows that if he can bring us into a place of fear, that fear will immobilize us so that we can be more easily beaten. When we retain the peace of God in those situations, however, we can see from a heavenly perspective, even in the midst of the worst type of attack. By simply choosing to allow His peace to rest upon us, even the most difficult situations will not overcome us.

Some time ago I went to the city of Baltimore to partner with some friends for an outreach in one of the local parks. Baltimore is a city that has gone through great tragedy and poverty throughout its history. There are real struggles with addiction and alcoholism all over town. In fact, the local team who lived in the area told me that people were getting so drunk before they went to work or on their lunch breaks that the city issued a special ordinance for particular areas, limiting the sale of alcohol to certain times of the day.

Our outreach took place on a cold day in November. We brought hot meals and warm clothing for all ages, set up some lawn chairs and invited people to come and let us bless them with prayer. We asked if anyone needed bodily healing or freedom from addiction, inviting those individuals to come and sit so we could pray for those who responded. At one point I happened to be standing by one of our prayer chairs when a gentleman named Michael walked past us. Michael looked like a regular guy wearing a nice leather jacket, a Bluetooth headset in his ear and a branded golf cap. He was just strolling through the park. As he walked by, he looked over at me and said,

"Hey, what are you guys doing here?" When I mentioned that we were praying for people, Michael asked if I would pray for him.

He told me that three years ago he had suffered a stroke that had impacted the right side of his body. Then he took his right hand out of his pocket and showed me how it was curled up like a claw. Since the stroke, he had not been able to open his fingers or use his hand properly. He then told me about his drop foot. He was unable to pick up his right foot when he walked, which was why he walked with a cane, dragging his foot behind him.

I invited Michael to close his eyes, and I prayed a simple prayer, asking the Holy Spirit to come and manifest healing in Michael's body. I blessed his body, thanked God for the healing power that was present and commanded the nerves to grow in the name of Jesus. Then I commanded the muscles in his hand and leg and foot to be strengthened. Led by the Holy Spirit, I then did something I had not done before. I put my hand above his head and said, "I command all chaos to leave, and I speak the peace of God over your body, in Jesus' name." The whole prayer was short and simple, no more than twenty seconds long. When it was over, I asked Michael to check out his body and see if he noticed any changes.

Slowly, Michael started to flex the fingers on his paralyzed hand, and all of a sudden, his fingers went from a tight claw to being fully spread out. He began to open and close his fingers over and over again, and when he realized he had been healed, he started shouting, "Oh my gosh, oh my gosh, what did you do to me? What did you do to me? Who are you? Do you have a card?"

"I don't have a card," I replied. "I'm a Christian. And Jesus loves you."

When I saw what had happened to his hand, I thought surely God had healed his foot as well, so I asked him to check out his foot. As he did so, he realized it was absolutely restored as well. His foot was healed! Michael began to wander around, slightly bewildered as the reality of what had just happened dawned on him. Then he started going up to total strangers, flexing his totally healed hand, putting it right in front of their faces and saying, "Look at my hand. Look at this!"

Finally, Michael retreated to a bench and for about forty minutes he sat and then stood, sat and stood, over and over again, just to make sure his foot was actually healed. I went over to him and said, "Michael, do you want to know the God who healed you today?" What followed was a "What must I do to be saved?" moment. It was so easy to bring Michael to Jesus that day.

Power Encounters with Peace

It is my belief that there needs to be an encounter for people to stay in the Kingdom of God. It is easy to talk someone into the Kingdom and just as easy for them to be talked out of the Kingdom, but it is nearly impossible to talk someone out of a power encounter with God. Whether it is an encounter where they feel the conviction of the Holy Spirit, feel His presence knocking on the door of their heart, a healing that happens in their physical body or a prophetic word that speaks life over them, encounter changes everything. Michael had just encountered God, and it changed everything for him.

When I pray for people, at some point I will ask them if they are feeling anything, such as heat or electricity, in their body. Oftentimes people will respond, "No, all I feel is peace." God's peace is actually a conduit through which His healing flows. One day I was teaching on the power of God's peace when a woman came up to me and asked me to pray for her grandmother who was at home dying of cancer. She was too sick to come to the conference. Because I was not able to leave the meeting, I agreed to pray from a distance, knowing from Scripture that God can heal through us whether or not we are present with the person receiving prayer (see Matthew 8:13; John 4:46–54).

The woman called her grandmother from the service and handed the phone to me. I introduced myself, shared a little bit about the biblical basis for healing and asked if I could pray for her. She was eager for prayer and immediately stated her willingness to agree with me in prayer for her healing. I prayed in Jesus' name, speaking His peace and life into her body, commanding cancer cells to die. I continued to pray and then asked her if she felt anything happening in her body, such as tingling or heat. "No," she said. "Just peace."

When I visited that church again about nine months later, the granddaughter could not wait to tell me that all the cancer had disappeared from her grandma's body. The doctors did not know what happened. This elderly, frail woman whose body was ravaged by cancer to the point of death had fully recovered, and the doctors had no explanation outside of a miracle.

Over the years I have asked friends, many of whom were third-generation Christians, "How did your family come to know Jesus?" Ninety percent of them replied that either their grandfather or grandmother was powerfully touched at a healing or revival meeting, and then the whole family got saved. Encounter brought them into the Kingdom— not good preaching or apologetics alone. I have traveled to many Muslim nations with the message of the Gospel. If I were to say to them, "The Holy Bible says . . . ," it would not hold any weight because they have their own holy book that says something different. But when God heals the sick, when words of knowledge or prophetic words are spoken over them that no one would know except God Himself, then they are open to hearing what the Bible says about Jesus.

When we read through the gospels, the book of Acts and the rest of the New Testament, it is not hard to see that encounters with God built the early Church from a few ragged, persecuted followers to a thriving body of believers in every part of the known world. God is still building His Church today through power encounters. It is important to preach and teach the Word, but we need Word *and* Spirit in order to see the Kingdom of God advance on the earth.

Several years ago, on one of our many trips to Brazil, Randy Clark and I became acquainted with a woman who we will call Miranda. She had stage-4 cancer and was dying. The cancer was throughout her bones, and there was nothing more the doctors could do for her. They sent her home to hospice care. When her family heard that Randy Clark was in town, they asked if we would come to their house and pray for her. When we got to her house, there was Miranda, in a hospital gown as she lay in a hospital bed. She did not look good. Randy went to one side of the bed, while I went to the other side. I typically keep my eyes open when I pray to see what the Father is doing, but this time I closed my eyes because I just wanted God to come. As I stood there praying, I felt a wind across my face. We were in a closed room—no windows were open and no fans were blowing. When I opened my eyes, there was Miranda, sitting up in bed, crying. We asked her what she was feeling, and she said, "I don't know. I just feel waves of peace going through my body." It was such an unusual experience that I believed Miranda was healed as we prayed.

A few months later, after chasing down Miranda's progress through our friends in Brazil, we found out that she was back to work and there were no signs of cancer in her body. She was totally healed by God's powerful peace. When God was healing her, Miranda did not experience heat or electricity in her body. She just felt the peace of God.

At least half the people I pray for do not feel anything at all except peace. I used to think that meant we had to pray some more in order to get results, because I thought that peace was the absence of anything happening. But now I know that peace is powerful. Peace actually manifests itself in the presence of God, often as a sign that He is healing a person. The power of God's peace overcomes external circumstances like a raging storm, as well as internal circumstances like cancer raging through a person's body. Where we think there is no answer, God has an answer, and often it comes in the form of peace.

▪ PRAYER FOR PEACE ▪

Father, help me to be a person of peace. Help me to experience and live in Your peace in the most chaotic of circumstances. I pray that the fruit of Your peace would grow so much in me that whenever I face chaotic circumstances, the peace of God that passes understanding would flow out of me. Help me to experience the richness of Your peace in the depths of my spirit and then help me to give it away to others. I have freely received Your peace today, so help me to freely give it to everyone I meet today. In Your name, I pray. Amen.

▪ 8 ▪

The Spirit of Peace

Then God blessed the seventh day and sanctified it,
because in it He rested from all His work which God
had created and made.

Genesis 2:3 NKJV

When the book of Genesis was written, it was a declara-
tion of who God was to the Israelites and a proclamation
of the God of Israel to the surrounding nations in the
ancient Near East. These nations had their own stories
to help give shape to their pagan gods and to explain the
world around them. For example, the creation narrative
found in our Scriptures has many similarities to other
non-Christian narratives. The story of our God, however,
is far superior to the common texts of the day.

Take, for instance, one of the pagan creation narratives
that taught that the world was born out of the blood of a
god who was defeated in a war of gods. The Hebrew text

from that same time period does not talk of gods in the plural at war with each other; rather, the biblical narrative speaks of just one God who reigns over all. He did not fight to create the world; He simply spoke it into being. The Genesis creation narrative proclaims the superiority of the one true God over all other so-called gods.

Genesis 2:3, when understood in the context of the time and culture in which it was written, gives greater clarity to who God is and what He was doing. It also gives us more clarity as to whom He created us to be in relation to Him. It states, "Then God blessed the seventh day and sanctified it, because in it He rested from all His work which God had created and made" (Genesis 2:3 NKJV).

When God rested, He did not just go back to heaven only to rest on a throne. His point of creation was to be with us, and to rest would be to rest in us or with us. If we miss this point from the beginning of the Bible and the beginning of creation, we may miss one of the biggest points of the Scriptures. John Walton writes, "What any ancient knew and few modern readers realize is that divine rest takes place in a temple. In the ancient world as soon as 'rest' is mentioned in connection with God, everyone would have known exactly what sort of text this was: gods rest in temples, and temples are built so that gods can rest in them."[1]

When humanity fell into sin, the wages of that sin were not just expulsion from the Garden of Eden and the ensuing limitations on our physical life on earth. It was much worse than that. Because of the Fall, we lost our position as temples or resting places for God. God's Spirit would no longer take up residence and rest among us and in us.

When the Spirit of God was with the Israelites during their wandering years, they had to build a traveling altar and the Tabernacle as a resting place for God's presence (see Exodus 26:14). The Spirit of the Lord would inhabit that Tabernacle as a physical sign of a cloud and fire (see Numbers 9:15–18). It was not until the life, atoning death and resurrection of Jesus took place that things shifted back, but in a slightly different way.

After Jesus ascended into heaven, God's Spirit was poured out on the disciples on the Day of Pentecost. Once again, God's Spirit would inhabit His people. And it has been that way ever since. God was always supposed to rest on us and with us. When we understand that the Spirit of God is with us and inhabits us as His temple, then we can live a revelatory life with God as He originally intended (see 1 Corinthians 3:16–17).

The *Paraklete*

> And I will pray the Father, and He will give you another Helper, that He may abide with you forever.
>
> John 14:16 NKJV

The Holy Spirit is essential if we are to live an authentic Christian life, especially regarding peace. The Spirit is so essential, in fact, that Jesus instructed His disciples to wait for "the gift my Father promised" before going out to minister and evangelize in His name (Acts 1:4). If they were to be effective witnesses for Jesus, then they had to be empowered by the Spirit. They were not to go in their own strength or with just what they had learned from Jesus; rather, they needed a present helper to abide with them.

In John 14:16, as Jesus comforted His disciples, He explained His plans to continue to care for them and be present with them after the crucifixion, telling them that God the Father would send the Holy Spirit to be their helper. The Greek translation of the Holy Spirit is *paraklete* or *parakletos*, which means helper or sanctifier or one who empowers. It is not limited to these words, however. The word in its plainest form means the One who comes alongside with whatever we need. For example, He can be a healer for those who need healing, an advocate for those who need justice or peace for those who are restless or troubled.[2]

Now, in context, we can weave Jesus' prophesying the coming of the Spirit and His purpose into John 20:21, where Jesus suddenly appears to His disciples in a locked room and says, "Peace be with you!" Understandably, they are startled and afraid that the man they saw crucified, dead and buried is suddenly standing in front of them. In verses 21–22, John records something that we do not find in Luke. Jesus speaks peace over the disciples, and then He says to them, "'As the Father has sent me, I am sending you.' And with that he breathed on them and said, 'Receive the Holy Spirit.'" I do not think Jesus just stood there and blew in the general direction of the disciples when He "breathed on them." I picture Him going to each one in turn and saying, "Peace to you," and then blowing on each man individually.

These verses in John are the last place in Scripture where we find the breath of God blowing on people. The story of humankind begins with God breathing His Spirit into the first man, Adam. In the beginning, the Father took the dust of the ground and formed Adam. Then, He breathed into his nostrils the breath of life, and the man became a living being (see Genesis 2:7). Those Hebrew disciples in the Upper Room would have been well versed in Old Testament Scripture. They would be familiar with the creation story, and because of their experiences with Jesus, they knew who He was—the Son of God. They also knew the great chasm of separation between humanity and God because of sin in the world. They had witnessed the brutal punishment of Jesus on the cross. In their minds, they thought the roller-coaster ride of the last three years was over. Yet there they were, just three days after His death, huddled fearfully in a room, when suddenly their Lord appeared in the room, resurrected.

It was then that all He had taught them began to fall into place. The great chasm between God and humanity was now filled by the love of the Savior. As Jesus stood among His disciples, declaring peace and breathing on each one of them, they may have thought of the creation narrative—of how God created Adam and Eve in the Garden. Now, in that moment with the resurrected Jesus, their own hearts were filled with life as His peace was deposited in them.

A Deposit of Peace

Jesus desires that you have His life, and that you have it in abundance. He wants you to have His peace, because His peace is powerful. When Jesus fills you with peace, that peace is transferable. What do I mean by this? Paul wrote, "May the God of hope fill you with all joy and peace as you trust in him, so that you may overflow with hope by the power of the Holy Spirit" (Romans 15:13). A deposit of peace causes us to "overflow with hope by the power of the Holy Spirit."

I have experienced transferable peace and a transference of anointing and watched in awe as God allowed me to give it away to others. Traveling with Dr. Randy Clark for over four years afforded me ample opportunities for impartations from him and others. Every impartation has had a significant impact on my life. One in particular, however, was so dramatic that it is worth telling as a way to encourage others that there is more peace in the Lord that can be experienced.

In February of 2014, I was released by Dr. Randy Clark to host my own conferences at Global Awakening. I prayed that God would give me His vision for these conferences, and He was faithful. He directed me to focus on renewal and the baptism of the Holy Spirit. I decided to call these conferences The Stirring, which was based on 2 Timothy 1:6: "For this reason I remind you to fan into flame the gift of God, which is in you through the laying on of my hands." I know what you are thinking—my last name is Martini and God has me doing conferences called The Stirring. Honestly, that humorous connection did not cross my mind at first. But now I often open Stirring Conferences with, "Welcome. My name is Paul Martini. I'm always stirred but never shaken." It is corny, I know, but I still do it.

In July of 2014, three days before my thirty-third birthday, I was conducting a Stirring Conference. I had invited

Blaine Cook to be one of my guest speakers. Back in 1994, God had used Blaine to light the spark of revival in Randy Clark's small Baptist church in Ohio. What ensued was a mighty outpouring of the Holy Spirit that burned all the way to Toronto and beyond, and is still burning today.

In charge of the conference, I had my manager/facilitator hat on and was busy with a myriad of details, making sure everyone was comfortable and having a good time. When it was time for Blaine to speak, I made the introduction and then handed the service over to him. Blaine came onto the stage, and before he started, he said he wanted to pray for the group from Pittsburgh. The Pittsburgh group had come to town specifically for The Stirring Conference. Blaine prayed for them, and God blessed them, sending every single one of them gently to the floor where they remained as the Holy Spirit touched them. Then Blaine said that before he started his message, he wanted to pray for all the intercessors. *Great*, I thought. I was championing all that was happening.

My wife is an intercessor, so I pushed her forward to receive prayer from Blaine. I did not want her or anyone else to miss out on a touch from God. I was so busy taking care of everyone else that I did not think of myself as all this was taking place. With the intercessors assembled up front, Blaine asked everyone to extend their hands and join him in praying. I was all in with what God was doing through Blaine. Standing there on the front row, I extended my hands and began to pray. Someone came up to me and touched me on my shoulder, and suddenly I felt a powerful touch from the Holy Spirit. I fell to the ground. It felt like electricity was flowing through my body. Powerful and almost painful surges of God's manifest presence kept causing me to hunch over. God had taken me by surprise with one of His "suddenly" moments. I did not know what to think.

God, what are You doing? I prayed. There I was, the one who was supposed to be in charge, so powerfully touched by God that I could not even open my eyes. I could barely stand. As if that were not enough, Blaine came and stood over me, laid his hands on me and kept asking God to give me more. Heat overtook my whole body like a vortex, causing me to shake uncontrollably. There I was, hunched over, shaking, sweating, with such powerful surges of electricity running through my body that I could hardly stand it. "Lord," I said, "I don't know what You're doing, but I want all You have for me."

Over the next couple of hours, person after person prayed for me as God continued to pour His power into me. People spoke words of prophecy over Ruth and me. Some came and held my hand and fell under the power of God. The heat on my body was so intense that I was soaked. My clothes were wringing wet as if I had just jumped in a pool, despite the fact that the air conditioning was on. I lost track of time. Blaine did not give his message that night, but God sure did. People were getting powerfully touched all over the room. After midnight, many people were still there, soaking in God's presence.

A few weeks before this experience, I had been in Georgia at a church called Higher Ground conducting a series of meetings in which I taught on healing, the peace of God and impartation. My impartation services had never been very powerful up until that point. God was using me powerfully to teach and heal, but when I ministered impartation, not much happened. Not much, until after the God encounter with Blaine Cook in July, that is.

My next conference was in Florida. I was preaching, but the message was falling flat and felt powerless, so I decided to stop preaching and just invite the Holy Spirit to come. "If you want the fire of the Holy Spirit, come forward," I told the crowd. Almost all of the four hundred people in the room quickly came to the front. I placed my hand on the first gentleman, and he flew back three rows of chairs and lay on the floor receiving powerfully from God. After that, the meeting exploded. The fire of God fell on most of those in attendance. We ran so late that they had to close the room and send us out into the lobby, where we remained for another two hours as I prayed for more people. I had never seen so many receive a touch from God through my hand. Since then, I have seen the revival fire of the Holy Spirit poured out on many people. God did not just release to me an experience that night; He gave me a commissioning to impart gifts to the Body of Christ.

My life has not been the same since that powerful impartation. I have grown tremendously in my ability to move with the Holy Spirit. I am more able to hear the Lord and follow where He is leading in a meeting. My preaching and teaching have become much more effective. Most of all, I feel like a tool sharpened and upgraded for a greater capacity of the anointing of God's Spirit. The fruit continues to grow in me in significant ways. I have seen deaf ears open, people on life support and with no hope come back to life and even the crippled start to walk. All of this brings more glory to Jesus Christ, taking worship of our Savior to a whole new level. I am so grateful for all that God has done and continues to do.

That night of impartation felt like Jesus breathing on me and saying, "Peace to you! Receive the Holy Spirit."

Fruit to Be Given Away

God wants us to bear fruit for His Kingdom. In fact, He is quite specific about the kind of fruit He desires. Galatians 5:22–23 (NKJV) says, "But the fruit of the Spirit is love, joy, peace, longsuffering, kindness, goodness, faithfulness, gentleness, self-control." These fruits are a by-product of His Spirit at work within us. As our relationship deepens and our intimacy with God grows, so the fruit in our lives becomes more plentiful.

Once, when I was praying and meditating on the peace of God, He showed me a picture of a fruit basket. In America, if someone calls you a fruit basket, it is not necessarily a compliment. That person is saying that you do not have it all together, maybe that you are a bit crazy. But that is not the only meaning of a fruit basket in our culture. When someone is not feeling well or is sick or grieving after a loss, we often put fruit in a basket, wrap it up and deliver it to that person's home. When I think of a fruit basket in those terms, I hear the Lord say that His fruit is not just for me, but that it is for others also. We all have fruit in our lives to share and to give away. Yet, if fruit goes unpicked, it gets overripe on the branches of the tree and falls to the ground, where it rots and goes to waste.

When I slice open an orange and squeeze it, orange juice comes out. If I squeezed an orange and apple juice came out, then I would find it odd indeed. Oranges should produce orange juice, and apples should produce apple juice. As Christians, we should also find it odd if fear, doubt, worry, stress and anxiety come out of us when we get squeezed. When the pressures of this world are upon us or the attacks of the enemy come at us, more peace should come out of us, not less. When we are under pressure, more peace, more joy, more hope and more love should be released.

It is possible to walk into a place of despair, a place of chaos, a place of hopelessness, a hospice or a hospital bed, and lay a hand on someone and have the peace of God transfer from your life and flow into theirs by the Spirit of the living God, along with His joy, love and hope. Scripture says that out of the overflow of our heart the mouth speaks (see Luke 6:45). God wants to flow into our hearts today with His peace, so that we let it flow out of us into the lives of others. "May the God of hope fill you with all joy and peace as you trust in him, so that you may overflow with hope by the power of the Holy Spirit" (Romans 15:13).

■ PRAYER FOR PEACE ■

Jesus, give me a desire to experience more of Your peace in my daily life. I thank You that I cannot live an empowered Christian life without the gift of Your Spirit. Holy Spirit, empower me with Your peace. Help me to live as a disciple of Christ, bringing the presence of God's peace to every situation in which I find myself. Make me hungry to receive from others so I that can experience more of You and be a more effective witness in my home and at work. Empower me with Your peace today. I pray this in Jesus' name. Amen.

9

Pitfalls to Peace

"The thief comes only to steal and kill and destroy;
I have come that they may have life, and have it to
the full."

John 10:10

Most of us will, at one time or another, find ourselves in
difficult and challenging situations. Just because we are
followers of Jesus and empowered by His Spirit does not
mean that we are immune to living in this world. Pitfalls
to peace are common. Just ask my friend Nathan Joudry.
I will let him share his story with you in his own words:

The story of Jesus raising Lazarus from the dead found
in John 11 intrigues me, as I know it does many others who have pondered this powerful Scripture. Raising Lazarus from the dead was a pivotal point in Jesus'
ministry, yet in one sense Jesus seems almost nonchalant
about the death of His friend. He receives the news that

Lazarus is gravely ill and close to death, but He delays His journey to Bethany for two days. Then, when He arrives, instead of going straight to Lazarus, who has now passed, Jesus, knowing He is going to raise Lazarus back to life, spends time with Martha and Mary, the sisters of Lazarus. I have come to the conclusion that Jesus is more interested in being a friend first and a hero second. Being the hero took a backseat to His relationship with Martha and Mary.

When He arrived at their home and saw their grief and distress, His heart was moved to first comfort them and mourn with them. Scripture says that Jesus cried with Martha and Mary. He was not crying about the death of Lazarus, since He was about to raise him back to life. I think He was crying because of His love and compassion for Martha and Mary. The Passion Translation puts it this way, "Then tears streamed down Jesus' face" (v. 35). Jesus, the hero of the story, showed up not just to be a hero, but first and foremost to be a friend. He did the same thing for me in a most difficult season of my life.

Several years ago, my wife and I planted a church in Asheville, North Carolina. Not long after that, things began to change. Unaware, I was embarking on one of the most difficult journeys in my life. It was on this journey that I first met Paul Martini and heard his message about peace. The message was profound and impacted me at my core.

We were about six months into the church plant, which was proving to be one of the most difficult things we had ever undertaken in our years of ministry, when our life began to unravel. My beautiful wife of eleven years asked me for a divorce. I was devastated. Our marriage was not amazing, but I never saw divorce coming, not in a million years. My first response was to dig in my heels and pray for my marriage and our two daughters.

As the days and weeks dragged by, it was all I could do to get up in the morning. I would drag myself out of bed, put on worship music and pace the floor in our living room. Over and over again, through tears, I would say to my soul, "God is good. God is good," until I believed it enough to get through the day. I have no idea how I wrote and preached a sermon every week. Those few months felt like an eternity. God was with me, crying with me, just like He did with Martha and Mary. It was His peace and friendship that got me through this time, until He showed up as the hero.

I began asking those closest to me, outside of the church, to pray. My father asked Paul Martini, whom I had never met, to pray, and he did. Paul had been in a similar situation. God ordained our paths. Then, Paul invited me to be his guest at a Stirring Conference he was leading for Global Awakening. I went, desperate for God to work in my life, unaware that God was setting me up to experience Jesus as hero, friend and the Prince of Peace.

On the second night of the conference, Paul shared his story. His struggle, vulnerability and pain resonated deeply with my soul. As we stood in worship the third night, the words of the song and the music pierced my heart, and I began to cry. It was not just a few tears trickling down my face. It was big, ugly crying. I remember falling into Paul's lap as he prayed something into my ear. Then I fell on the floor, where I remained for the rest of the three-hour service, until Paul picked me up and put me in the car.

I had no idea the extent to which God was working in my life that night, and that what He was doing would carry me through in ways I did not expect. After this significant encounter with God, I thought things would get better at home, but that was not the case. In fact, they got much worse. My wife was having an affair with a family friend. When his wife found out, she gave my wife an ultimatum: "Tell your husband or I will." My wife left work "sick" that morning to tell me about the affair and that our marriage was absolutely over. She was done.

I remember the devastation, the fear, the anger, the hurt and the sense of betrayal as I sat on the couch in our living room. I also remember the Prince of Peace, tangibly sitting next to me on the couch as tears streamed down my face. I believe they were streaming down His face, too.

I left the house to go for a drive, to process the overwhelming thing that was happening and to pray. I called Paul on the phone, and he ministered the peace of God to me.

Arriving home, I found my wife upstairs, where I calmly looked her in the eyes and said, "I love you. I forgive you. I honor you. You are my wife and I honor you." I don't know why I said those words. I do believe God set me up for that moment during my encounter at The Stirring Conference. He set me up to experience His peace in the darkest moment of my life.

The scales fell from my wife's eyes that day. Suddenly she could see with fresh revelation just what she was doing, who she was hurting and all that she was losing. She told me she didn't want a divorce. She wanted to fight for our marriage and our family.

That day, peace came to my heart and my house, not just to be a hero, but to be a friend. You see, the Prince of Peace was with me on the worst days of my life when all I could do was muster up enough strength to say, "God is good," until I believed it enough to make it through the day. The Prince of Peace was with me when my wife shared the worst news I've ever received. The Prince of Peace made a way for our journey to complete restoration of our marriage.

Now, years later, our marriage is amazing. We have experienced the peace of God that passes all understanding. His peace now rules and reigns in our home. Our church is growing and experiencing the presence of God in new ways. The Prince of Peace healed our hearts, sat with us, saved our marriage and our ministry.

Paul Martini likes to say, "The God of peace sent the Prince of Peace to bring the Gospel of peace." It is true! Peace came and now lives in us.

Nathan Joudry, pastor, Ridgeline Church, Asheville, North Carolina

Get Out of the Boat

Our lives are complex, and we do not have the answers to all the questions that arise. So often we do not see clearly when looking for direction. Many times, we do not even know where to begin or where to look for peace. Since I am an itinerant minister who teaches on peace, many people come to me asking for help, wanting to know how to get to a place of peace or just how to start on the journey. I find that speaking from experience is what helps them the most. I tell them that when I found myself in a dark place, I tried to account for all the reasons I was there. Was it just unfortunate circumstances or unlucky breaks, or was it because others had wronged me? It was not until I stopped thinking my woes were someone else's fault and realized that I needed to begin by looking at my own actions that things began to change.

When I was struggling through my divorce, I remember being on my bed pleading with God for some sort of break or favor from Him. In the midst of my pain, God took me back to a memory from when I was a young boy, reminding me of my words to Him. "God," I had said, "I want to have a heart like Yours to follow You and do whatever You ask of me." Those words were heartfelt, but as I grew up, I stopped following God and started living life my way, engaging in some risky living while pushing God entirely out of the picture. God did not leave me behind. I left Him, because a life of sin is not compatible with God. Yet, when I was battered by the storms of life and cried out for His help, God in His mercy took me back and showed me His path to life with him. *Paul*, He said, *it's time to get out of your boat.*

I did not fully understand what He meant until a few months later.

I was in California and had a message planned and was ready to preach it when I heard the Lord firmly say, *Not that message, Paul. I want you to tell the people to get out of the boat.*

"O God, not another message about Peter," I moaned.

No, not another message on Peter, He said. *I want you to preach on Jonah.*

Suddenly, I knew where God was going with this. One of the greatest evangelists in the Bible was a prophet who was stubborn and did not want to obey God. Jonah's disobedience put him in a place where he and others suffered.

Jonah was like any other prophet in his day: He would hear from the Lord and proclaim God's message to the people. That is, until God gave Jonah a message he did not want to pass on.

God had a message for Jonah to give to the people of Nineveh. The problem for Jonah was that the people of Nineveh were evil, and he did not feel like they deserved a warning from God to repent and be saved. Jonah had a decision to make, and he chose poorly. He chose to do what he wanted to do and not what God called him to do. In hindsight, it is easy to be critical of Jonah, and yet many of us make Jonah-decisions all the time without even realizing it.

Jonah did not do anything horrible. He did not curse God or give a different message to the people. He just bought a one-way ticket in the opposite direction of Nineveh. To Jonah, it must have seemed like a good decision at the time, until all hell broke loose. There he was, with his ticket, in a boat, heading away from Nineveh when a terrible storm came upon them. The captain of the boat found Jonah asleep and running from his problems. "Wake up, you sleeper!" he cried.

Many of us are at one time or another asleep in the boat during the storms of life, ignoring what God is telling us to do. Called out for his disobedience, Jonah advised the crewmen to throw him overboard so that the boat would not sink. They obliged. Jonah found himself in the raging sea, where God sent a large fish that promptly swallowed the disobedient prophet. All was not lost, though. After three days in the belly of the whale—how is that for a chaotic experience?—Jonah was spit out on shore and made the wise decision to do what God asked of him.

If you are going through difficulties and crying out to God for help, allow Him to take you back to that moment when you took life into your own hands instead of being obedient to Him. Are your storms the result of your own bad choices? If so, allow Him to get you back on track, even if it means spending three days in the belly of a whale. If you want His peace, you have to put on His shoes of peace and walk on the path He has set for you.

When I submitted my life to God and committed to follow wherever He leads, I found that He not only started to bless my life's decisions, but He actually inserted Himself into my circumstances, becoming my advocate even when I stumbled. God is not interested in beating us over the head with our mistakes. He does not hand out suffering for our wrong decisions. He is waiting eagerly for us to return to Him, take His hand and walk with Him in the cool of the Garden.

Received with Loving Arms

I made the decision to rededicate my life to God, yet things did not change right away. Or should I say, I did not change right away. As a result, I continued to experience the consequences of living a life of disobedience to Him. I made selfish, unwise decisions that led to suffering. In my confusion, I expected God to treat me accordingly. But that is not in the nature of God. It is His kindness that leads us to repentance. To my surprise, God said, *Paul, I'm with you. I'm here to help you out of these difficult circumstances.* I was so relieved even though I had no idea how

God was going to move on my behalf. I was so thankful, just knowing He was with me.

In addition to bad life choices, I also made some bad financial decisions during my time of brokenness. I remember getting a letter in the mail one day from the IRS saying I owed them $13,000. I did not have $1,300 to my name, let alone $13,000. Unable to afford an accountant, I had done my own taxes the year before and had obviously made a mistake. I was distraught, to say the least. Anxiety flooded my brain until God reminded me that He was with me in the storm. As God and I discussed the situation, He responded to all of my it-is-impossible scenarios with His assurance that He would get me through.

The letter from the IRS said I had thirty days to respond. I decided to wait a couple of weeks to respond so as to pray and listen for God's wisdom and direction. Before the thirty days were up, another letter arrived from the IRS. This one said that they had made a mistake. I did not owe them $13,000. I only owed them $1,300. Dumbfounded but so grateful, I called and set up a payment plan of $25 a month, thanking God the whole time. I never mentioned my IRS issue to anyone—my family, friends or church group. To my surprise, a short time later a check arrived with a note from someone I had known for only a brief time. It said, "Paul, God is with you. He told me to send you this money." It was the exact amount I needed to finish my payments to the IRS.

What does all this tell us? It tells us that God truly is for us, not against us. If you have strayed, return to Him with all your heart and expect to be received with loving arms.

Do not let the years you strayed stop you from accessing God's peace today. He is for you and not against you.

Convinced of God's Goodness

Often, even though we are presented with the goodness of God by God Himself, we go through our lives unconvinced that His goodness is true for us. Sure, it is true for other people, we believe, but surely it is not true for *us*. This is another pitfall of accessing and releasing the peace of God.

There is a correlation between chaos and an unconvinced mind. When our mind is not convinced of the real character and goodness of God, then it becomes an open door for the enemy to plant seeds of disbelief. When we continue in a mindset that doubts the goodness of God, the seeds of unbelief will choke out whatever fruit of peace has grown in us. You might be reading this book with a hope that God is good—and I am glad for that—but that hope needs to turn into a real faith that God actually *is* good.

Your faith is the soil that nourishes the seeds God plants in your heart. Seeds have difficulty growing in dry, rocky soil. They need rich soil, plenty of water and lots of sunlight in order to survive and thrive. When you allow God to nourish the soil of your heart with the water of His Spirit and the light of His Son, you create an environment that is ready and able to receive whatever God gives.

When Jesus was baptized, the heavens opened and the Holy Spirit descended on Him like a dove. God spoke, "This is my Son, whom I love; with him I am well pleased"

(Matthew 3:17). The Father audibly and publicly blessed Jesus, and then the Holy Spirit drew Him into the desert, where He fasted for forty days and forty nights. This time of testing was so difficult that Jesus needed angels to minister strength to Him before He was able to leave. While Jesus was in the desert, Satan tempted Him with the very word that was spoken over Him: "*If* you are the Son of God . . ." (Matthew 4:3, 6, emphasis added).

God the Father had just declared that Jesus was His beloved Son in whom He was well pleased, and here was Satan challenging the very words of the Father. The word God spoke about Jesus was the word Satan challenged Him with. If Satan would challenge Jesus in this way, then he will challenge us in a similar manner. The moment we get the revelation in our spirit and God speaks His peace over us is the moment all hell will try to break loose in our lives. The devil is afraid of the words spoken over us by God and wants to challenge us to abandon them.

I cannot tell you how many times God spoke peace over my life, and then the moment I left an amazing worship service or devotional time, life blew up in my face. It could be as simple as someone cutting me off in traffic or a family member getting upset and taking it out on me. It is a strategy of the enemy trying to provoke us into a place where we accept the storm in front of us instead of staying in the mindset that what God said is true, and this is only a test to see whether or not we will believe it.

When we receive His peace, we need to be prepared for the enemy to attack us. How do we prepare ourselves? We need to keep our focus on Jesus and not on our circumstances, remembering His response when tempted by

Satan. In the face of Satan's lies, Jesus quoted the Word of God: "Man shall not live on bread alone, but on every word that comes from the mouth of God" (Matthew 4:4). Jesus made the choice to listen to His Father in heaven and not the father of lies. Choose to believe the Father who speaks life and light over you more than the lies of the one who comes from behind to steal, kill and destroy.

Demonic Strongholds

Another pitfall that prevents us from accessing and releasing God's peace is our understanding of demonic oppression. As Christians, we should recognize that we have the right to be free from all oppression, including demonic oppression. It is not the children's bread. Matthew tells a story about Jesus healing a woman's daughter who was demonized and suffering terribly. When Jesus blessed the woman's daughter, however, she was healed and became whole from her demonic suffering:

> A Canaanite woman from that vicinity came to him, crying out, "Lord, Son of David, have mercy on me! My daughter is demon-possessed and suffering terribly."
>
> Jesus did not answer a word. So his disciples came to him and urged him, "Send her away, for she keeps crying out after us."
>
> He answered, "I was sent only to the lost sheep of Israel."
>
> The woman came and knelt before him. "Lord, help me!" she said.
>
> He replied, "It is not right to take the children's bread and toss it to the dogs."

"Yes it is, Lord," she said. "Even the dogs eat the crumbs that fall from their master's table."

Then Jesus said to her, "Woman, you have great faith! Your request is granted." And her daughter was healed at that moment.

Matthew 15:22–28

I travel throughout the world and see Jesus setting people free from demonic oppression throughout South America, Asia and Africa. But when I travel the Western world, it seems as though people do not deal with demonic oppression any longer. Some people would think that all the demons are overseas, but this is simply not true. The demonic influence is just as prevalent in America as in any other nation. The problem is that we call it different names, such as anxiety, depression and obsessive-compulsive disorder.

Surely there are natural causes for all sorts of issues, but demons often go undetected by blaming natural causes and symptoms for our state of demonically inspired dysfunction. All across American Christendom, there are churches full of people who need freedom and wholeness, but we have forgotten that this is our right as children of God.

Sometimes the peace we lack is from a demonic stronghold in our lives. These strongholds can come from numerous sources, such as trauma we have experienced, habitual sin we are stuck in or even bad theology we have believed. But we need to understand that peace and freedom are synonymous in the Kingdom of heaven. If we are bound by demonic oppression, then how can we experience true peace?

Let us first recognize that we might have a problem that comes from more than mere natural causes, such as mental or physical causes. Then, let us look at the supernatural that is behind such symptoms. Take authority over your life and come against the possible demonic stronghold in your life. Ask God for His peace to break the strongholds and command the enemy to leave your body.

After rededicating my life to God, I still struggled in one particular area of sin. For me, it was so strong that if I did not actively fight it every day, then I would fall. I would get a lot of momentum and everything would be going well for a season, but then I would fall back into that sin once again. It was like the devil knew that if he could not get me in one area, then he could always try to knock me out of peace through this one sin. All other temptations were easy to say no to, but this one area had a hook in me. I used to blame myself for a lack of discipline and was always hard on myself, which brought me into seasons of despair.

Then the Holy Spirit pointed out that this could be more than a temptation or lack of discipline—it could be something even more sinister, such as a demon. I was taken aback by this thought. I thought a Christian could not have a demon. Did this mean that I was not saved? What was God saying? The reality was that I believed in all the Christian creeds and had a personal relationship with Jesus Christ, so I knew I was born again. The issue was that I had a parasite (i.e., a demon) that tried to go undetected and brought me into a place of compulsion, which meant I was not free in this one particular area.

Jesus told us in Matthew 7:7 NLT, "Keep on asking, and you will receive what you ask for. Keep on seeking, and you will find. Keep on knocking, and the door will be opened to you." The New Living Translation emphasizes the continuous nature of the verbs in the original Greek. Sometimes we ask once and think God is not there, but He really expects us to repeatedly knock and ask and seek. Jesus also told a story about a man who came to his neighbor in the middle of the night asking for bread and would not take no for an answer. If the neighbor would arise and give him bread because of his persistence, then how much more would God give us what we ask for when we are persistent (see Luke 11:5–8)?

When I read this, I thought, *I'm going to keep knocking until I get an answer, until I get freedom.* So, I started persistently praying for freedom from this awful stronghold day after day. About 21 days later, God answered me as the power of the Holy Spirit filled my body and I began to shake. I did not realize what God was doing at the time, but I said, "God, if this is You, then do what You need to do." I began to cry profusely because I realized that God was touching me. Then I did something I had never done before: I laughed and laughed and laughed. I was in my room by myself crying, laughing and shaking under the power of God. This went on for nearly an hour.

Even though I didn't immediately realize it, when I got up from that experience, I was free from my bondage. This does not mean I was never tempted again, but I felt like I had a choice from that point on—I had freedom from the Holy Spirit to say, "No, I don't want that." It was true freedom and peace that was brought about by breaking the demonic stronghold in my life through the power of the Holy Spirit. Even though the enemy tried to keep me from accessing and releasing God's peace in this one area of my life, as I prayed to break demonic oppression, I experienced a level of freedom I hadn't known before.

Taking Inventory

Take a few moments for self-reflection. Take inventory of areas where you find yourself stuck in a rut. Are all the issues natural causes or something more than the normal issues in life? Is it possible that your struggles could be from spiritual torment, a stronghold or an afflicting spirit? If you are not sure, then it might be good to say some prayers and deal with a possible spirit afflicting you.

Much like doctors who run many tests if they do not see what the issue is at first, so we need to use prayer as a tool to treat the root causes of what may be afflicting us. If you are still struggling and nothing seems to work in breaking free from that stronghold, then pray for deliverance over your life. You have nothing to lose . . . except possibly a stronghold. Do not let the pitfalls of peace keep you from accessing and releasing God's peace in every area of your life.

▪ PRAYER FOR PEACE ▪

Heavenly Father, I thank You for Your love for me and the price Your Son paid for my salvation and deliverance. I pray Your blessing and protection over me today. Please guide me in all truth by Your Holy Spirit. I take authority over any evil spirits that are influencing my life, and I command them to come out in the name of Jesus. I command every spirit that is from the kingdom of darkness to leave my life right now. Father, come and fill me with Your Holy Spirit and empower me to walk in freedom. I ask that You equip me and anoint me to cast out demons and set the captives free. Let nothing hinder me from accessing Your peace. In Jesus' precious name, I pray. Amen.

10

The Wisdom of Peace

But the wisdom that is from above is first pure, then peaceable, gentle, willing to yield, full of mercy and good fruits, without partiality and without hypocrisy. Now the fruit of righteousness is sown in peace by those who make peace.

James 3:17–18 NKJV

After the breakup of my first marriage, I quit thinking about marrying again and got busy with the Lord's work as an itinerant minister, traveling the world with Dr. Randy Clark and Global Awakening. But God, in His wisdom, had other plans for me.

Each year, Global Awakening conducts a three-week summer intensive. Attendees come from all over the world to be taught and learn from some of the generals of the faith. That particular summer, however, one attendee caught my eye and my heart. I did not know it then, but love was about to come into my life and set up camp in a big way.

Ruth Stewart had come to the summer intensive from Australia. There was something different about her. Over the three weeks she was at Global Awakening, our hearts started to connect, and then she was gone, back to her life in Australia. We were diligent about staying in touch, however. Thank goodness for technology that eases the strain of long-distance relationships. Through Skype and social media, we got to know one another and became good friends. As our friendship and eventually our love grew, we struggled to make sense of what it would look like if we were to seriously consider marriage.

I was a single dad who traveled a lot and did not have a significant source of income to provide for a wife and family. Ruth was busy with family, career and her church in Australia. It would have made sense for each of us to move on from the relationship and continue to go our separate ways. We were both happy with our respective lives, yet God was doing something special in our hearts.

Our many discussions kept bringing us back to one thing—we both felt a great and constant sense of peace about our relationship and thoughts of a future together. We knew that bringing our two busy lives together in marriage from half a world away would not be easy, and not everyone in our lives was totally supportive of the idea, but our intent was pure. So, we decided it was wise to follow the peace of God that was on our circumstance. Out of all the doors before us, we chose the peace door.

The Peace Door

I began visiting Australia as often as I could, and then it happened—I asked Ruth to marry me. And she said yes! It was time to close the great physical distance between us and become husband and wife. We set about figuring out the myriad of details involved in bringing her to the States for our wedding. She needed a visa, of which there were several options. There was the fiancée visa. To obtain one of these is an intense and challenging process, which takes a long time. Then there was the tourist visa. It offered a quicker option, but there were greater risks attached to it. For starters, we would have to marry quickly, and Ruth would have to begin the green card process after the fact. The risk with this option is that Homeland Security has the option of denying someone a green card. When that happens, the person is immediately deported. Most of the people we knew in similar situations had chosen the tourist visa, but we decided to pray and wait to hear from God.

Often, I do not get a specific word from the Lord when I go to Him with a major decision I have to make. Instead, I will get a sense of direction and a familiar feeling of peace. This peace is not due to the fact that I have chosen the less challenging option; it is simply God's way of letting me know I am in His will for that particular situation in my life.

Out of our separate prayer times, there emerged a peace about the fiancée visa, so we decided that was the route for us. We were told that fiancée visas typically take three months to obtain. Ours took over a year, despite all of the paperwork and evidence of our relationship. We were heartsick, yet God's peace did not leave us. In hindsight, the delay proved beneficial to Ruth and me. She was able to tie up the loose ends of her rich and full life in Australia and organize her departure with ample time to say proper good-byes to family and friends. Plus, I had time to wrap up my commitments to Dr. Randy Clark.

As hard as that year was for the both of us, when Ruth's fiancée visa was finally approved, we had peace about her status from then on. Since that time, all major decisions in our life have to pass the peace test. We have learned that being sensitive to God's peace in a situation is a wonderful way to process life.

Peace in Our Decisions

One of our favorite Scriptures on peace is James 3:17–18. There is a progression of God's wisdom in this passage and its relationship to His peace. It begins with purity characterized by a personal agenda yielding to the will of God. Hearts and minds set on God's will above all else are happy and peaceful hearts. When we lay down our earthly goals and pick up His goals with pure hearts, then we are sure to find the wisdom of His peace.

I love how James highlights the peace of God as wisdom that comes from above, a gentle willingness to yield that is full of mercy and good fruits, without partiality or hypocrisy. He goes so far as to say that the fruit of righteousness is sown in peace. God intends that we are not anxious about anything, "but in everything by prayer and supplication with thanksgiving let [our] requests be made known to God; and the peace of God, which surpasses all understanding, will guard [our] hearts and [our] minds through Christ Jesus" (Philippians 4:6–7 NKJV). Ruth and I aim to live these words of Scripture, because we know it is the only proven path for our life.

Surrendering God's peace for what seems like gain is not the option we choose. It is not an easy path, and I will not pretend that we are not tempted to veer off at times. And to be honest, we sometimes do veer off, and the results are always predictable. I do not believe God intends for us to cease to care about the necessary things of this world. In fact, I would suggest that this is a lack of wisdom. We are to give attention to what needs to be done, make our needs known to God, trust Him and participate in this life according to His will.

Anytime there is a decision that Ruth or I need to make, we try to allow time for prayer and sitting before the Lord before we make the decision. It is not that we do not make decisions when they arise; we have just learned that God's peace is a great way to govern our life decisions. If we have spent time praying about a certain situation, even if the opposite decision makes more sense in our minds, we go with the peace of God. Since God is aware of all the variables of a given situation, we trust that He knows what is best in every situation and what will happen down a certain path. And God backs this up with His peace.

Peace should be present in your heart when making a significant decision. Even if it is a courageous situation that you are stepping into that is difficult or unfamiliar, if His peace is resting on you, then you can face it without allowing its enormity to influence you. When the Israelite spies were sent to spy out the land of Canaan, there was much to be seen (see Numbers 13). All the spies saw the same rewards in front of their eyes—a land flowing with amazing promises. They also saw their biggest potential enemy—the giants that possessed the land.

Encountering a situation with natural eyes and factual circumstances alone is shortsighted and even deadly. You will mostly likely only see the biggest object right in front of you. But when you look with the eyes of peace, this allows you to perceive the supernatural power of God's potential in the situation. Moving toward a decision in the mindset of peace will reveal where the peace of God is in that situation.

The spies who were moved by fear, and justifiably so, were immobilized to apprehend what God promised them, but the ones who could see the promise of God above the fear would be able to report in peace. This is often how I try to live my life. I do not just juggle life decisions based on logic alone. I try to look at them with the mindset that fear will have no place in my decision and that God's peace will remain. Often, when I can look at a situation with God's peace resting on me, I can see it more clearly and sense the direction that the Lord is pointing me in. The next time you have to make a major decision, spend time waiting on the Lord and learn to discern His peace.

Sowing Peace

James 3:18 points to a principle of Kingdom living that is a significant aspect of God's will—sowing peace. What does it mean that "the fruit of righteousness is sown in peace by those who make peace" (NKJV)? We are made righteous in

Christ Jesus, and the fruit of that righteousness should be a peacemaker's heart. The heart of a peacemaker is always drawn toward opportunities to interject peace into a given situation, whether it is by promoting or celebrating others above yourself or by adopting a position of peace in a difficult situation, even when it means you lose ground.

A few years ago, I was speaking at a large international event alongside some generals of the faith. As a young minister, I was honored to be invited to take the same stage with these mighty men and women of God. I carefully and prayerfully prepared my message, asking God to move in the hearts of the people when it was my turn to speak. My heart was overflowing with thankfulness at the opportunity to minister, and I was excited to think that this might open doors for me. Family and friends were cheering me on.

God always knows how best to work on issues of the heart, which is what He did for me at that conference, in an unexpected way. I had not yet had an opportunity to speak when the event coordinators called all of the speakers together for a special meeting. They had inadvertently not allowed enough time for one of the main speakers to share and were stressed about their error. They asked if anyone was willing to give up a session. I was the only unknown minister in the group, and it seemed obvious to me that I should be the one to step aside. But I was torn.

Part of me knew it was the right thing to do, but the other part wanted more than anything else to take that stage. I had traveled so far, sacrificing time away from my wife and children, and I had prepared so diligently. The issue they were struggling with was not my fault. Honestly,

I was so disappointed I felt like crying, and I probably would have if other people had not been around. I knew what I had to do. My choices were to stay right with God and give my spot away, or go with what I wanted and let someone else deal with the issue. Knowing righteousness is sown in peace, I gave my session away. The organizers were grateful to be able to extend to this prominent speaker additional time, and those in attendance were blessed as well.

Determined not to let my disappointment turn into wisdom from below that promotes self, I set my heart on the wisdom from above that loves peace. As it turned out, later in the conference, one of the speakers was able to give me a portion of his night session. He invited me up on stage to share my heart, and God moved powerfully in our midst. All things really do work together for good for those who love the Lord and are called according to His purpose (see Romans 8:28).

Remember that peace is not seen or heard—it is action. There will be important moments that will be begging for us to sow peace into by bringing wholeness or an answer to a need. It could be a crucial moment of our lives that we can identify and sow into, but we need to expand our thinking beyond significant moments.

When we sow peace, we should sow with an ancient mentality. What do I mean by this? Modern farmers sow seed by placing a seed in a perfectly punched hole in the ground. It is a perfect example of how we think in our society—everything is supposed to be placed perfectly in order for it to work. When the Scriptures speak of sowing, however, it is in the context of the Eastern world. We have to remember that they were sowing seed before farming was industrialized. Farmers in Jesus' time would sow by having a pouch tied to their side and would grab a handful of seed and walk the fields waving their handfuls of seed, making sure the seed scattered everywhere.

When we walk through our daily lives, we need to be situationally aware of where we can sow peace into moments in any given day. It is easy to be oblivious of the areas that need peace in our surrounding environments. As we go throughout our day, we need to think of ourselves as farmers with a bag of peace attached to our hips, sowing peace to all that is around us. We have the answer the world has been waiting for. Do not wait for a single moment to sow peace—spread peace wide and spread it intentionally.

Promoting a Life of Peace

If we are to walk in the wisdom that God supplies, wisdom that comes from heaven, then we need to be people who seek to remove jealousy from our hearts and do all that we can to stay pure toward others, thus promoting a life of peace. James reminds us that if we give place to jealousy, then we are we are not promoting the wisdom of peace at all but rather a wisdom that comes from below:

> Who is wise and understanding among you? Let them show it by their good life, by deeds done in the humility that comes from wisdom. But if you harbor bitter envy and selfish ambition in your hearts, do not boast about it or deny the truth. Such "wisdom" does not come

135

down from heaven but is earthly, unspiritual, demonic. For where you have envy and selfish ambition, there you find disorder and every evil practice.

James 3:13–16

James tells us that if we truly have wisdom, then we will show it by our "good life, by deeds done in the humility that comes from wisdom." The peace of God will not reign where there is "bitter envy and selfish ambition." That is a type of wisdom, James says, but not the type that is becoming of Christians. That kind of wisdom is "earthly, unspiritual, demonic." When envy and jealousy are present in our hearts, there will be disorder, which only comes because of a lack of God's peace. If we truly are to be the peacemakers God invites us to be, then we should seek to have pure motives and rid our hearts of the sin of jealousy.

There are so many emotions that can rise to the surface when things do not go the way we want them to. Jealousy was one of those for me. Early on in ministry, I struggled as another young minister rose through the ranks more quickly than I did. It seemed like I was constantly comparing the two of us, thus trying to justify my feelings. I thought I worked harder, was more experienced and better suited, and, therefore, I deserved more favor than he did. When we see favor on someone's life, we usually do not know the full backstory. We do not know everything that person went through before God's favor came upon him or her.

It is amazing how quickly our thoughts can go downhill when emotions take over. Jealousy is not from the Lord. It is a trap of the devil. Thankfully, the Holy Spirit crashed in on my negative, ungodly thinking and pointed me in the right direction with His wisdom. He showed me that the best way to fight jealousy is to celebrate those who are experiencing God's favor—what James calls "deeds done in the humility that comes from wisdom."

When we meet jealousy with peace, we engage the kind of upside-down thinking that so often characterizes the Kingdom of God. Wisdom from above is always peace-seeking and peace-loving.

As I thought about how I would want someone to celebrate me, and what that would look like from a peace perspective, I began to overflow with ideas of how I could celebrate this fellow minister. I started to recommend him to all the pastors I knew. I shared about him on social media. I prayed for him and his family, sent them gifts and invited them over for dinner. All the while, I did what I could to ensure my heart was pure toward him. As God's peace settled on the situation, everything shifted. We became good friends. He started to extend his favor toward me. We were no longer competitors. We now love to work together to see the Kingdom advance on the earth. Instead of celebrating ourselves, we celebrate Him, the One who is worthy of it all.

Jesus promises us, "But seek first his kingdom and his righteousness, and all these things will be given to you as well" (Matthew 6:33). As we seek God's Kingdom first and put away jealousy from our hearts, then we can move in the wisdom of God's peace. The wisdom that God invites us to walk in has a supernatural dimension of peace to it: "But the wisdom that comes from heaven is first of all pure; then peace-loving, considerate, submissive, full of mercy and good fruit, impartial and sincere. Peacemakers who sow in peace reap a harvest of righteousness" (James 3:17–18).

Let us be people who walk in the wisdom of God's peace, becoming peacemakers who sow in peace and thus reap a harvest of righteousness.

▪ PRAYER FOR PEACE ▪

Dear Jesus, please come now and be my peace. I put my life in Your hands, yielding to Your wisdom in all things. Help me to see all of my circumstances through Your lens of peace. I know that if I trust in Your wisdom and strength and not my own, I will find contentment. Please rid my heart of all jealousy and help me to have pure motives so I can walk in the peace that You provide. Holy Spirit, give me the wisdom that comes from heaven, wisdom that is peace-loving and kind and gentle. Help me to put away selfish ambition and envy, so I can walk in Your peace with pure motives. I pray all of these things in Your name today. Amen.

▪ 11 ▪

The Prince of Peace

For to us a child is born, to us a son is given, and the government will be on his shoulders. And he will be called Wonderful Counselor, Mighty God, Everlasting Father, the Prince of Peace.

Isaiah 9:6

Isaiah 9:6 is one of my favorite go-to Scriptures on Jesus, the Prince of Peace. It is a beautiful, poetic passage that gives us one of the most stirring pictures of our Lord and Savior in all of the Bible. In stark contrast to Isaiah's description of Jesus being the Prince of Peace is John's description of Satan as the father of lies (see John 8:44). While Jesus is all about giving us His peace, Satan is busy trying to destroy that peace. Jesus said, "The thief comes only to steal and kill and destroy; I have come that they may have life, and have it to the full" (John 10:10).

The enemy of our souls is not necessarily worried about our gifting or our anointing, or the special talents we may have. He is not prowling around looking to burn down every church building on the planet. All he needs to do is steal our peace. Without God's peace in our lives, we become ineffective for the Kingdom of heaven. Have you ever tried to lead someone to Jesus when you are anxious? Or when you are in a hurry to be somewhere else and running short on time? Or just after you have been arguing with someone? You cannot lead someone to the Prince of Peace when you are not walking with Him. Unless His sovereign grace is in operation, it is hard to function well without His peace.

Why Are You Afraid?

In the gospel of Mark, we find the story of Jesus and the disciples crossing the Sea of Galilee. In Jesus' time, there were three modes of transportation—walking, riding a donkey or a horse and sailing in a boat. Boats were a common mode of transportation and essential to the livelihood of many people. We often find Jesus on or near a boat in the gospels. In this particular story, the disciples are frightened as they cross the sea, but Jesus seems more interested in teaching them than calming their fears.

> That day when evening came, he said to his disciples, "Let us go over to the other side." Leaving the crowd behind, they took him along, just as he was, in the boat. There were also other boats with him. A furious squall came up, and the waves broke over the boat, so that it was nearly

140

swamped. Jesus was in the stern, sleeping on a cushion. The disciples woke him and said to him, "Teacher, don't you care if we drown?"

He got up, rebuked the wind and said to the waves, "Quiet! Be still!" Then the wind died down and it was completely calm.

He said to his disciples, "Why are you so afraid? Do you still have no faith?"

They were terrified and asked each other, "Who is this? Even the wind and the waves obey him!"

Mark 4:35–41

Whenever I am reading Scripture and come to a place where Jesus is interacting with the disciples, I slow down so that I can look for the deeper meaning, the nuances of the language, in order to better understand what Jesus was showing the disciples in that moment. Knowing the context of the time is important to understanding the full scope of the story. I want to know what is happening and discover what Jesus is truly teaching, because He is demonstrating how we, as His modern-day disciples, are to live on the earth, understanding who we are and whose we are. This particular passage resonates with me because, over the past few years, I have traveled a lot via airplane to get where I needed to go.

In my first year traveling with Randy Clark, I flew about 200,000 miles. These days I fly about 150,000 miles a year. I would call myself an experienced flier, or maybe even a professional flier. People think international travel is glamorous, and maybe it is for the first couple of months. But the reality is that sitting in a chair for nine hours at 35,000 feet is not fun at all. Those who travel a lot just get used to navigating airports and the long hours on a plane.

I am generally peaceful when I am flying because I know that, statistically speaking, flying in an airplane is one of the safest modes of transportation. There are thousands of flights every day, and we hear of one plane crash every couple of years. Flying is actually much safer than driving in a car.[1] Since I understand that, I am not usually bothered when we hit turbulence. It is just a change in air pressure that can cause the plane to shake and bump around a bit. Sometimes I will look around during turbulence and notice a man whose hands are gripping the armrests until his knuckles turn white, or a woman who is crossing herself, and I think, *Ah, isn't that cute? He must be an amateur flier. She thinks we're actually in danger.*

But when I see a flight attendant get anxious—when I see him or her getting people out of the restroom and back to their seats, making sure everyone is buckled up—then I begin to worry, because flight attendants are professionals. They are the flight experts. When I see them get concerned, I start praying in my prayer language, calling for angels under the wings of the plane, and getting my Bible out and ready to give my last salvation message if we start to go down.

Several of the disciples who were in that boat crossing the lake with Jesus were experienced professional fishermen, rugged men who knew what it was like to be in a storm that is so strong and violent that they might die. Their experience of what could happen created a natural fear in them. The thing about fear is that when it gets inside of you, it spreads like wildfire. The only thing that makes you feel better when you are afraid is making sure the person next to you feels afraid as well. If everyone else is afraid, then we feel better about being fearful ourselves. It somehow validates our fear.

I can easily imagine what was happening in the boat—experienced fishermen were getting more and more anxious as the wind got stronger and the waves got higher. As the noise of the storm increased, the boat would have been taking on water due to the massive waves crashing over the sides. Boats sink in that kind of a storm. The disciples' reaction was to cry out, "Jesus, this is an extremely fearful moment. We are all afraid, and You should be too. Don't You care that we are all about to die?"

If any moment in life deserved a fearful response, it was certainly this one. There they were, in a little wooden craft, being tossed about like a rag doll on large waves, a great windstorm blowing so loudly that they could barely hear one another speak. Then there was Jesus. He was in the same boat, in the same storm, fast asleep. When the disciples woke Him, He did not respond in fear. Instead, He stood and faced the storm and released the peace that was inside of Him to overcome the storm. Bill Johnson put it this way: "You have authority over any storm you can sleep in."[2] Jesus released the peace inside of Him with a simple decree of authority, and the raging storm surrounding them became calm in a moment.

How to Handle Fear

It is possible to take this passage of Scripture and interpret it to mean that the peace of God will carry you through the storms of life. God's peace will sustain you, even when your life seems to be at stake. This is a biblically correct interpretation of the meaning of this passage. In fact, we find it in Psalm 23, where David writes, "Even though I walk through the valley of the shadow of death, I will fear no evil, for you are with me; your rod and your staff, they comfort me" (v. 4 ESV).

While there will be times when you will need the peace of God to sustain you as you are going through a storm, that is not what Jesus was teaching during that moment. If it had been, He would have demonstrated how to live in that moment, saying something like, "Okay, guys, let's get in a circle, hold hands and start singing Psalm 23." Then turning to Simon, He would have said, "You pray, and let's agree together for our safe passage across the lake." But that is not what He did. What He said at the beginning of their journey gives us a clue as to what He was going to teach them in the midst of the storm: "Let us go over to the other side" (Mark 4:35).

Before they ever got into the boat, Jesus told His followers that they were going to the other side. This was not a faint impression or a vague idea. If Jesus only did what He saw His Father doing, then He had already seen them safely on the other side of the lake and was simply following His assignment from heaven. When He said to them, "Why are you so afraid? Do you still have no faith?" (Mark 4:40), He was pointing out that their fear had robbed them of their faith. When He had finished speaking to them, He demonstrated how to handle fear by speaking peace to the chaos.

On another occasion, Jesus stepped between a father who had faith that Jesus could heal his daughter who was at the point of death and a bad report that had brought fear into this father's heart and robbed him of the faith he previously had (see Mark 5). Jesus saw the initial faith of the father, which compelled Him to go to the man's house to see his sick daughter. But while they were on the way, someone came to the man to report that his daughter had died. "As soon as Jesus heard the word that was spoken, He said to the ruler of the synagogue, 'Do not be afraid; only believe'" (Mark 5:36 NKJV).

What was Jesus doing here? He was releasing a peace that guarded the heart and mind of the little girl's father. Even though someone from the house had come to tell the man that his daughter had died, Jesus released His peace with a word of hope. He did not want the bad news to allow fear to get into the heart of this faith-filled father and rob him of what he needed in that moment.

When they finally arrived at the house, Jesus only allowed those with faith—the mother and the father and the disciples—into the room with Him where their daughter lay dead. Then, just as He had spoken peace to the storm, He told the girl to arise, and immediately she rose up. God's peace manifested itself to protect the faith of a mother and father and to bring their daughter back to life, just as it did in the boat during the storm.

The Prince's Authority

The royal attribution—Prince of Peace—that is used to describe and prophesy about Jesus has such significant meaning because it describes Jesus' authority as a ruler (see Isaiah 9:6). Whether Jesus was in that boat or He was with the little girl's father, He was not just allowing circumstances to dictate the authority He walked in. Instead, Jesus brought peace, and, as such, was using His authority to reclaim ground and tell the world that the place where He was walking was under His authority. As a result, peace abounded in that place.

Likewise, when we walk in the authority of Jesus Christ, we enter areas as His ambassador and with His authority, giving us the right to claim areas for Him. When we do this, we shift a circumstance from a realm of chaos and disorder to an arena of peace. When the Prince of Peace is present, thus causing peace to reign, His power flows easily because it is like His heavenly Kingdom is making contact with earth. This is another reason Jesus taught His disciples to pray "your kingdom come, your will be done on earth as it is in heaven" (Matthew 6:10).

My friend Richie Seltzer and I were in Brazil preaching at a church. We taught on different aspects of healing all weekend long, but I also emphasized the peace of God in that process. Throughout the weekend, there was a church member there who had a condition called spastic paresis, which did not allow her to walk. She was in a wheelchair. The last night, Richie and I both led a miracle service. Many people were healed that night. Tumors disappeared, calcified bone bumps on a leg vanished, a blind woman regained her sight. It was a fabulous night.

Toward the end of the night, the woman in the wheelchair was carried out of her chair and was brought to the front of the church, where she lay on the floor. Even though many prayed for her that night, this dear lady was not healed. She would try to stand up and just fall back down to the ground again. Over and over again, she tried to stand up, but nothing changed. Richie could see her grimace each time she tried to stand, so he asked her if she was in pain. She confirmed this and motioned for her wheelchair to be brought back. It was getting late. She started to accept that this might not be her night to be healed. Then something strange happened.

A crowd of young people surrounded her and started to sing about no one stealing God's glory, for all glory comes from Him and goes back to Him. Richie felt compassion for her and hugged her. Then he quickly prayed for her legs and he stood up, closing his eyes to worship in song with everyone else. At that moment, the woman tried to stand one last time. As she did so, power came into her legs, and she ran up on the stage and started jumping. It was an amazing miracle! Everyone present was touched.

The Prince of Peace was present that night, and it did not seem like anything was going to hold back His Kingdom from coming on earth as it is in heaven. While many prayed and many were healed, only God gets the glory. All her chaos, pain and difficulty finally came to an end that night when we exercised the authority Jesus gave us to declare His peace in this world. We are able to access and release God's peace because we have been given Jesus' authority.

Authority as Ambassadors

God gives us the spiritual authority to bring peace to the different places we go and preach the Gospel. There are worldly peacekeepers and there are Kingdom peacemakers—the difference is in the spiritual authority of the one bringing the peace. Jesus' disciples went into the world preaching the Gospel of peace to all people, walking out their anointing as ambassadors for Christ (see Luke 10:1–24). You may not be called as a diplomat sent to avert wars between nations, but there are plenty of conflicts going on around you that are closer to home, whether they are within your family, your community, your church or your city.

I was traveling for three days speaking to a church on healing and the power of God's peace. I was scheduled to speak to a group of pastors and leaders the following morning, but the night before I received a frantic call from the pastor of the church asking me to forgo teaching the next morning and go to the hospital to pray for someone.[3] The pastor explained that someone close to him on staff had just been in a motorcycle accident and was fighting for his life.

I agreed to go but was a bit nervous to be thrust into a life-or-death situation. I have prayed for many people and have seen many healed, but I also see a lot who are not healed. No matter the outcome, it is important to remember who the healer is—Jesus Christ. Dr. Randy Clark likes to say that when he prays for someone and nothing happens, he can see what he can do; but when he prays for a person and sees him or her healed, then he can see what God can do. As I recalled Randy's words, my confidence for the situation increased.

Since the hospital was about an hour away from the hotel, I had time to press into the presence of God and receive His peace. When we arrived at the hospital, we entered the man's room where he lay in a coma with tubes and machines keeping him alive. His organs were shutting down. He had a machine helping his lungs breath and a machine for his kidneys. Organ transplant was a consideration—if his organs failed and acceptable donors could be found. On top of all this, he was battling an infection. Needless to say, seeing him in this state was a shock. My first thought was, *We need a miracle.*

Several staff from the church had come with me. As we stood there around the bed, we began singing a beautiful worship song. As our praises to God filled the room, the atmosphere began to change from fear, despair and hopelessness to peace, boldness and faith. I laid my hands on this man and started praying that the Lord would heal his body, make right his organs and stop any internal bleeding. The Lord gave me an impression to go over to him and speak life and peace into his ear. Even though he was unconscious, in obedience, I leaned over him and in a soft voice I said, "I declare peace and life over you. I speak life and peace into your body and declare that you will live."

As I finished speaking, his oxygen levels started to rise. The machines that were attached to him started beeping. Nurses rushed in. To everyone's surprise, all his levels were good once again. We continued to pray until it was time to return to the meeting; we were thankful and hoping for a miracle. Knowing he was not expected to last through the day, we were in continual prayer as we finished the rest of the conference.

I found out that a week later the man in the coma miraculously recovered and woke up with no side effects. He was so beautifully healed that he skipped the step between ICU and physical therapy. It was a true miracle indeed. The doctors could not explain his recovery except to say that his organs became alive again. God's peace took a man from the edge of death back to life. I saw him later that year at another conference looking vibrant and healthy. God gets all the glory.

No matter what you are facing today, Jesus asks you, "Why are you so afraid? Do you still have no faith?" (Mark 4:40). He is the Prince of Peace who speaks one word and causes chaos to cease. One word from God can change your life forever. He is the Prince of Peace who destroys all fear, who causes us to rest secure in His love and to walk in His authority. Because of Jesus' death and resurrection, He has become our peace, and we are now able to access and release God's peace into every storm we face.

■ PRAYER FOR PEACE ■

Jesus, I thank You that You are the Prince of Peace. When You show up, all chaos has to bow to Your powerful name. When You show up, all sickness and disease have to leave. I pray that You would come as the Prince of Peace in my situation today, speaking peace to the storm that tries to cause chaos all around me. Help me not to be robbed of the faith You have given me, and empower me to walk in the authority of peace You have graciously given. In Jesus' name, I pray. Amen.

A Prayer for Peace

God's peace is tangible, real and powerful. In Isaiah 61, God says that Jesus came to set the captives free and proclaim freedom for the prisoner:

> The Spirit of the Sovereign LORD is on me, because the LORD has anointed me to proclaim good news to the poor. He has sent me to bind up the brokenhearted, to proclaim freedom for the captives and release from darkness for the prisoners, to proclaim the year of the LORD's favor and the day of vengeance of our God, to comfort all who mourn, and provide for those who grieve in Zion—to bestow on them a crown of beauty instead of ashes, the oil of joy instead of mourning, and a garment of praise instead of a spirit of despair. They will be called oaks of righteousness, a planting of the LORD for the display of his splendor.
>
> Isaiah 61:1–3

If you feel like you have been robbed of your peace, if you are believing the lie that you will never find His peace again, then I speak freedom over you in Jesus' name. I ask the Holy Spirit to manifest that freedom right now in your life. I ask you to use your self-control to give God all control and to position your heart as if you are going to receive a gift. Pray this prayer today:

Holy Spirit, come now and have Your way in my heart, mind, will and emotion. Release the super-natural peace of God. Father, I thank You for this moment that You have ordained in time. Jesus, thank You for the peace You give me and for the peace You leave with me, so that my heart will not be troubled or afraid. Holy Spirit, I welcome You into my heart and life.

May Your peace be with me.
May Your peace cover me.
May Your peace fill me.
May Your peace bind any brokenness in my heart.
May Your peace heal the things
highlighted in my mind.
May Your peace mend that which
needs to be mended.
May Your peace guard my heart
and mind in Christ Jesus.
And may Your peace crush Satan under my feet.

In the name and authority of Jesus Christ, I rebuke every spirit of fear and torment, and I command it to leave me now and to go to the place assigned for it, never to return again.

I break the hook that the enemy uses to bring me back into moments of trauma. Father, I ask that You would heal the memory associated with the trauma and that all associated effects become null and void.

I come against restlessness and night terrors, and I break their power in Jesus' name. I speak the peace of God over those situations in my life, and from now on I will know peace through the night.

Finally, I say, peace to you. Receive the Holy Spirit.

Notes

Chapter 3: Peace Is Central to the Gospel

1. Michael J. Gorman, *Peace in Paul and Luke* (Cambridge: Grove Books, 2015) 5, 7–8, 13, 22, 23, 26. This is a booklet that was adapted from "The (New) Covenant of Peace," chapter 6 of Michael J. Gorman, *The Death of the Messiah and the Birth of the New Covenant: A (Not So) New Model of the Atonement* (Eugene, Ore.: Cascade, 2014). Gorman writes, "However, importance is determined not only by the quantity of texts, but also by such factors as their location, their connection to related words and themes in the author's corpus, their relationship to scriptural texts and motifs, and so on. Any or all of these could either reinforce or challenge an initial impression based solely on quantity" (*Peace in Paul and Luke*, 5).

2. Timothy Keller, "The Meaning of Shalom in the Bible," The NIV Bible, accessed February 1, 2019, https://www.thenivbible.com/blog/meaning-shalom-bible/.

3. "Sozo," *The NAS New Testament Greek Lexicon*, Bible Study Tools, accessed February 1, 2019, https://www.biblestudytools.com/lexicons/greek/nas/sozo.html.

Chapter 4: Growing in Peace

1. "Matthew 5:9 'Blessed are the peacemakers,'" Christ's Words in Greek, accessed January 16, 2019, http://christswords.com/content/mat-59-blessed-are-peacemakers.

2. Arthur Charpentier, "The U.S. Has Been at War 222 out of 239 Years," Freakonometrics, March 19, 2017, https://freakonometrics.hypotheses.org/50473.

Chapter 5: Living as Peacemakers

1. "Cleansing of the Temple," Wikipedia, accessed January 2, 2019, https://en.wikipedia.org/wiki/Cleansing_of_the_Temple.

2. "Matthew 5:9 'Blessed are the peacemakers.'"
3. "G1515—*ēirenē*—Strong's Greek Lexicon (KJV)," Blue Letter Bible, accessed January 2, 2019, https://www.blueletterbible.org/lang/lexicon/lexicon.cfm?Strongs=G1515&t=KJV.
4. "G4160—*poieō*—Strong's Greek Lexicon (KJV)," Blue Letter Bible, accessed January 2, 2019, https://www.blueletterbible.org/lang/lexicon/lexicon.cfm?Strongs=G4160&t=KJV.
5. "John 14:27 Peace I leave with you," Christ's Words in Greek, accessed January 2, 2019, http://christswords.com/content/jhn-1427-peace-i-leave-you.
6. Martin Luther King Jr., "'Loving Your Enemies,' Sermon Delivered at Dexter Avenue Baptist Church," Stanford University: The Martin Luther King, Jr. Research and Education Institute, November 17, 1957, https://kinginstitute.stanford.edu/king-papers/documents/loving-your-enemies-sermon-delivered-dexter-avenue-baptist-church.
7. King, "'Loving Your Enemies.'"

Chapter 6: Advancing in Peace

1. Michael A. Fletcher, "Harrisburg, Pennsylvania's capital, files for bankruptcy," *Washington Post*, October 12, 2011, https://www.washingtonpost.com/business/economy/harrisburg-pennsylvanias-capital-files-for-bankruptcy/2011/10/12/gIQAeQ6HgL_story.html?noredirect=on&utm_term=.8bce2b0d0645.
2. Diana Fishlock, "Cab driver killed in Harrisburg identified as a Steelton man," *Patriot-News*, PennLive, March 12, 2012, https://www.pennlive.com/midstate/index.ssf/2012/03/cab_driver_killed_in_harrisbur.html.
3. Clay Clinesmith, "Peace or Shalom," Hebrew Word Pictures, accessed January 16, 2019, https://www.hebrewwordpics.com/explain-peace/.
4. For more information about the Pax Romana, see the great book by Ali Parchami, *Hegemonic Peace and Empire: The Pax Romana, Britannica and Americana* (Abingdon, Oxon, U.K.: Rutledge, 2009).

Chapter 8: The Spirit of Peace

1. John H. Walton, "Reading Genesis 1 as Ancient Cosmology," *Reading Genesis 1–2: An Evangelical Conversation*, ed. J. Daryl Charles (Peabody, Mass.: Hendrickson, 2013), footnote on page 158. See Psalm 132:7–14 as additional supporting text.
2. For a great history about this word, see James Orr, ed., "Paraclete," *International Standard Bible Encyclopedia*, accessed January 31, 2019, https://www.biblestudytools.com/dictionary/paraclete/.

Chapter 11: The Prince of Peace

1. Aric Jenkins, "Which Is Safer: Airplanes or Cars?," Fortune, July 20, 2017, http://fortune.com/2017/07/20/are-airplanes-safer-than-cars/.

2. Bill Johnson, "You Have Authority Over Any Storm You Can Sleep In," Charisma News, September 13, 2014, https://www.charismanews.com/opinion/45352-bill-johnson-you-have-authority-over-any-storm-you-can-sleep-in.

3. I love to pray for the sick. Given a choice between praying for the sick or empowering leaders to pray for the sick, however, I would choose to empower leaders, thereby reproducing what God is doing. This was a hard choice for me.

Paul Martini, an associate evangelist with Global Awakening, travels the world extensively, training, teaching and imparting the gifts of the Holy Spirit. He has ministered in 35 nations and has preached on five different continents. Throughout his travels, he has seen blind eyes restored, deaf ears opened and the crippled walk through the healing power of the Holy Spirit.

Paul is a 2011 graduate of Global School of Supernatural Ministry and holds a B.A. from Phoenix University of Theology. Currently, he is obtaining his master's degree in theology from Global Awakening Theological Seminary. He has served Randy Clark with honor and humility, traveling with him for over four years. In addition to healing and evangelism, Paul's heart is to train and equip the Body of Christ to impact their environment and culture.

Paul is the director of events for Global Awakening and is the founder of The Stirring, There Is More, Hope Fest, and Rise conferences. He is truly blessed with his beautiful wife, Ruth, and, as of the time of printing, his six children: Giovanni, Giuliana, Shiloh, Freya, Oscar and Charlotte. He is based at Global Awakening's headquarters in Mechanicsburg, Pennsylvania.